SURRENDER

is good for the

SOUL

Surrender is good for the Soul -
The art of surrendering to gain fulfilment in life

Cover Design by Sally Page
Cover Photo by Annie Spratt

Visit www.boundless-meditation.co.uk

To the lost soul who wants to be found

Contents

Sur • ren • der

- Dictionary meaning -

To give up personal control for personal peace

Acknowledgments

My first acknowledgment is to my husband. He is a truly remarkable human being, kind, humble, loving and incredibly generous. I value the unconditional support I receive from him beyond anything words can express. He is always there for me in so many ways. His love and support are a beautiful foundation for me to fly free and create in this world.

Then I must give gratitude for our two children, who are now grown adults. Jasmine, our eldest, is a ray of sunshine and has been since she was born. She is kind, thoughtful, considerate, flamboyant and a huge inspiration for me. I am constantly amazed by her tenacity and willingness to keep going at the same time as helping those who need her support even when she is struggling herself. She is incredibly insightful, a shining example of using art to understand and process the inner workings of the mind and emotional expression.

Brodie is also kind and has a unique way of viewing the world which has made him an amazing and insightful teacher for me. He will not accept injustice or nonsense, and this has enabled me to say no when I used to say yes. He has shone a light of reason onto nonsensical societal ways we have grown accustomed to even though they no longer serve. Change must happen and he is so grounded in a kindness and acceptance of all human beings simply being themselves. I've always felt the same but have often shied away from standing my ground in this matter.

My mum is also an ongoing source of new realisations. Our relationship continues to grow in depth and compassion. She also proofread and edited this book for me, which was an enlightening education. I love learning new things and my love of books and vocabulary has been stimulated and expanded as a result of her notes and observations of my writing. Thanks Mum!

My gratitude will always go to my spiritual teacher Maharishi Krishnananda Ishaya who is an unwavering guide on my journey to wake up. The other Ishayas around the world are my wonderful companions on this path and I am forever grateful for their love, acceptance, and kindness.

My core values are honesty, kindness, and acceptance. The people I surround myself with have these values too. It's so important for me to be around people who lift me up and encourage me to be the greatest version of myself.

Thank you to all the people I meet who also demonstrate a kindness and openness to create this world anew in a more compassionate, loving, and sustainable way.

Thank you to you the reader, without your support I won't be able to reach people and share a new way of being. Life can be joyful, easy, and peaceful no matter what is happening in the world around us, and I want to demonstrate this is so with my books, courses, and talks.

Gratitude is a guiding principle which keeps my focus on what I want more of, rather than that which I want to remove from the world. This approach is far more direct and effective at cultivating beneficial change for the good of all. So, I'm grateful for gratitude itself!

Introduction

Surrender is often misunderstood, and we can feel like we mustn't ever surrender, because it means another person is ruling our life.

Surrender is not the same as giving in though.

Surrender is standing in our own power and being true to ourselves. It's a purification, so we can come back into our natural state of being.

Surrender is so much more than our perception often reveals. Thoughts and emotion colour our experience, so we're often in a battle with ourselves, oblivious to the harm we inflict on our mind and body.

We resist and battle against life so much and cause ourselves a huge amount of suffering. This battle and a need to win and feel valuable sabotages us again and again.

Surrender brings with it an end of resistance, an end to the pressure we so often call pain.

Emotions run riot when we resist, pain intensifies and thinking goes into overdrive with absolutely no respite. Whereas surrender is a beautiful and gentle way to respond and live our lives.

This book outlines all the ways we approach life and miss the truth because our mind holds onto an outdated opinion or belief.

Within these pages is an invitation to look again. To step back from the minds rambling thoughts and rest into stillness to re-cognise the pure, clear experience for ourselves.

This is surrender. It's a softening, a realigning with the Universal force for good.

It's so important to learn the art of surrender, so we can work with what life brings us. All that is required to learn the art of surrender is a shift in perspective and a willingness to try a different approach.

If you so choose, explore the suggestions I make, and discover for yourself what works best for you.

"The moment of surrender is not when life is over.
It's when it begins."

- Marianne Williamson -

Chapter 1
Theoretical Understanding

What does surrender mean to you?

For me, the experience and understanding of the word surrender has changed dramatically. I used to feel so worthless, yet I was also very angry. This led to a lot of words, people and situations triggering me left, right and centre.

The word surrender made me feel as though I had to give up and let somebody else rule me. I didn't like this idea at all. Even though I didn't feel good enough, I desperately wanted to be. I naively thought, that if I fought long and hard, I would never have to surrender to anyone. Nor would I relinquish control of any situation. I was determined to always find the best solution for me, and I would never give in.

This approach was obviously not sustainable. There were many situations which did not go my way. In continuing to fight against everything and everyone, I became exhausted, and fatigue set in. There was no choice left for me. I had to give up and let go of the outcome.

This wasn't surrender though. I zoned out, shut down, all hope lost. I became numb and resentful. I was held captive by my own mind and body. I couldn't even walk, and I was in an extreme amount of pain.

This approach wasn't sustainable either.

Thankfully help came. My life, my mind and my body gradually healed as I learnt an entirely different approach to life - surrender.

Surrender started to evolve into a direct, alive experience. My previous theoretical understanding of surrender changed over time. Surrender was no longer something to avoid at all cost.

However, for quite some time, surrender was still something I only understood theoretically. But as the theory began to change, so did the experience. In fact, it worked both ways - my understanding of surrender also changed because of the change in my experience.

Through practising Ascension (a meditation type practice) I started to relax and let go naturally and easily. The Ascension techniques did the job for me. I stopped needing to understand and work it all out. As I continued to use these techniques, what I needed started to come to me effortlessly more and more of the time.

Surrender became a way of life, rather than something I did or didn't do. Surrender for me is a very natural state of being. I didn't have to try to stop fighting against life.

Recognition of the simplicity and gentleness available to me began to light the way. As I started to realise that I could go with the flow of events, life became simple, easy and also much more fun.

Surrender is a light-hearted and gentle approach to life. As trust grew within me, surrender became much easier to choose. The more I was willing to surrender, the more good came my way.

I can't believe how hard I fought against the natural flow of life. I'm surprised I managed to cope for as long as I did! All the battling and forcing nearly broke me. But in truth I'm unbreakable. At the point I couldn't take any more and didn't want to continue on in life, a miracle occurred.

As I stopped resisting, space opened up for an entirely different experience. This expanded state of being, in turn, opened me up. Help and support, far beyond anything I could ever have imagined or hoped for, started to flow into my life.

Surrender is the way forward. True surrender is allowing ourselves to simply be, exactly as we are.

Surrender, in my experience, is the opposite of thinking, trying, or controlling. We have choices rather than control, and when we activate clarity, we are enabled to discern the best path forward in every situation.

Surrender is empowering. It allows us to tap into our natural talents and resources. The direct experience of surrender is sweet, gentle, and immensely powerful.

I use all the challenges in life as a signpost to freedom. As soon as I recognise I am resisting what is, I stop and surrender to the moment.

This acceptance of my current circumstances allows me the space and clarity to engage with the flow, and work with the hand which is dealt to me.

This has always led to a greater level of fulfilment and enjoyment of life for me. The direct experience of surrender far surpasses any theoretical understanding in my experience.

Surrender is the doorway to a rich, enjoyable, and fulfilling life. But don't just think about it! Thinking about surrender is not the same thing as applying it. Thinking about surrender can torment you and make you feel useless. You cannot surrender from the mind.

Surrender is best explored and engaged from stillness and silence. Simply by paying attention and allowing the way forward to present itself, can make life a whole lot easier.

I invite you to read on as I share my own experience and understanding of surrender and how to approach it most effectively.

"Thoughts are created by suppressed and repressed feelings. When a feeling is let go, thousands or even millions of thoughts that were activated by that feeling disappear."

- David R. Hawkins -

Letting Go:
The Pathway of Surrender

Chapter 2
A Thought Created Reality

Life is not what it appears to be. We have become so attached to the thinking mind; it governs every waking moment. We are basically experiencing everything through the filters of the mind.

If we identify with and believe what the thoughts in our mind say, we will experience what they tell us to experience.

This is why surrender can be so difficult to apply in our everyday life. Our beliefs about what everything means affect how we see, feel, hear, smell, taste, touch, and experience it. So, our concept of surrender, like everything else, is distorted.

When we decide to do something new, these thoughts held in the unconscious mind control how we approach it. We're not free to explore anything without the past conclusions affecting the way we explore.

It's almost as if we have a virtual reality headset on. We only see what we are programmed to see. The same goes for hearing, tasting, touching, smelling, feeling, and experiencing.

As long as we subscribe to these beliefs, nothing is experienced purely or clearly. Beliefs are just thoughts which are held to be true and downloaded into the unconscious mind. The thoughts play on repeat until we recognise what is happening and let them go.

Surrender is the mechanism by which we free ourselves to experience life without our past impressions governing how we experience it.

How do we do this? Well, I would say in order to stop unconscious patterns of belief affecting our understanding of reality, we need to raise our level of consciousness. We need to make everything that is unconscious, conscious.

We can't force this to happen. We will need to surrender to 'what is' so we can become more aware. Shine the light of consciousness into the dark, so we can see everything clearly.

Once we begin to see everything more clearly, the unconscious patterns dissolve. Everything which no longer serves us, falls away. The light of consciousness dispels the darkness of unconsciousness.

As we become more and more consciously aware of every thought arising within our awareness, we begin to recognise how false a lot of them are.

The light of truth shines forth and we automatically surrender, as we recognise what is real. Discernment and intuition grow, and the thought created reality fades away.

Simply paying attention with all of our senses in this moment will allow us to become more consciously aware.

Everything naturally comes back into balance and operates efficiently and effectively. Life becomes effortless because our body's innate intelligence and capacity to heal is unhindered.

Intuition takes over from thinking and guidance comes from the heart, which in my experience is always a more accurate compass.

Life is meant to be lived in surrender. Life is always working in our favour. We only get to see this is true when we are surrendered and allow what wants to happen, to happen.

In a state of surrender, all our words, feelings and actions are purified and in alignment with everyone and everything. We are free from all past experiences and can live in purity and joy.

It may be hard to believe this is possible, or even that it's true. I only know it's true by exploring surrender for myself and by continually surrendering to this moment.

Only by learning how to surrender and applying it to every aspect of our lives, are we able to recognise what is real, and what is just a thought.

To go beyond our own thought created reality is the point of being alive. Once we start to let go, we begin to find that life is so much easier.

Other people become much easier to get along with too. The clarity surrender brings, enables us to be creative, playful, and willing to listen to others. They, in turn, will begin to listen to us more and more of the time.

Humanity operates much more effectively as a team. Surrender allows us all to play our own part most successfully. Solutions are always available when we pay attention and allow them to arise. We may come up with the answer, or it may come from another source.

When thoughts no longer govern our perception, so much more becomes apparent and accessible.

If we want to see and experience the bigger picture and have access to all the opportunities available, all we have to do is surrender ... and keep surrendering ... for as long as it takes for clarity to arise.

I find it's helpful to always assume that what I know to be true is incomplete. This way I am open to everything and all I need comes to me.

This attitude means I don't waste energy trying to prove I'm right. Thoughts can always be colouring my understanding in each and every moment.

Be still, surrender, and pay attention. Then it's easier to see beyond our thought created reality.

"Too many people overvalue what they are not
and undervalue what they are."

- Malcom S. Forbes -

Chapter 3
There's Something Wrong

There's something wrong.

This is the biggest lie in the history of everything! The idea that there is something wrong with us, our life, or anything, is the fundamental belief that creates a sense of wrongness in our lives.

Everything that goes wrong is sabotaged by this underlying belief. This is not to say there are things that aren't dysfunctional and need to change. But if we want to facilitate effective change, we first need to let go of the idea - 'there's something wrong'.

Why? Because it is false and harmful. If we are so focused on what is wrong, we tend to miss out on all that is right and good in our world.

When we surrender this false belief, change is more likely, not less likely. Positive change.

As we stop running this idea in our mind, it creates space for intuitive solutions to arise in our awareness. We also free up energy to enable us to put a solution into action and facilitate a more functional and peaceful environment for us all.

If we hold on to this belief in something being wrong, or right for that matter, our perception of life will unfold according to whatever our mind dictates is right or wrong.

Holding on to this belief, or any belief, causes friction and pressure within us. It prevents surrender and the natural flow of energy is restricted. Life becomes incredibly forceful, and suffering occurs.

The belief that there's something wrong creates the feeling that there _is_ something wrong. It's very convincing and 'feels' true. But just because it 'feels' true, doesn't mean it _is_ true. A feeling can be deceiving.

It can often take a leap of faith to go beyond this convincing belief and accompanying feeling. It takes courage and tenacity. But it is always possible.

We don't need to live like this. There is another way. We can step past immediate appearances and go beyond our current perception to access an entirely different and more functional world view.

I invite you to drop the idea that there's something wrong and look at every aspect of your life through fresh eyes.

What is really happening? And ... regardless of what appears to be happening, get quiet and still... then ask - what wants to happen?

And watch ... pay full attention ... and notice what you are aware of right now.

Notice what you can see ... Notice what you can hear... What else are you aware of?

Notice, then keep exploring ... What else? ... What else?

In this exploration surrender happens.

Just this easily and naturally we let go … and we simply rest … present to this moment. Alert and aware of what unfolds as it occurs.

This is all it takes. The idea that there's something wrong fades into the distant background and we are open to new possibilities, new opportunities.

What's this like?

Explore … and keep exploring … see what you discover in this new operating mode. Sure, the mind will kick back in and try to run the show again. It's a habit. But that's all it is - a habit.

If you want to explore this some more, I recommend you find an effective tool to retrain your focus away from the limiting beliefs in the mind.

The most effective techniques I've discovered are the Ascension Attitudes as taught by The Bright Path Ishayas. You might want to try them out for size. More details about these techniques can be found in the resources section at the back of this book.

Whatever you choose to try, or not try, know this: there's nothing wrong with you and you have all the answers you need within you. You may need some help or guidance accessing them, but they're there, hidden in plain sight.

Everything you ever need is accessible to you.

All you've got to do is look with clear vision and listen with open ears … and … surrender.

"When you're angry, you're just a character in someone else's story. When you let your anger go, you reclaim your own story, become your own protagonist again."

- Inventing Anna -
(A Netflix series)

Chapter 4
Anger and its many disguises

Anger is a very destructive force. Anger used to rule my life. I spent most of the time on gentle simmer. I appeared relaxed, but I was on edge and ready to blow up at any moment.

There were so many things and people who triggered me, I could barely make it an hour without flipping into a highly reactive state. This is no way to live. I was incredibly stressed, anxious and irritable.

Anger can be hidden really well by some people. They appear calm and their voice remains steady and at a quiet level. However, there is a tension that can be sensed by those of us who are more sensitive to pent up emotion.

I found it really difficult with those who were what I would call passive aggressive. The controlling behaviour and manipulative nature of these types of people used to drive me insane.

I was unable to handle the devious and underhand methods people like this used to get their way. I completely lost all sense of self and became buried in a ball of simmering white hot rage. I found myself doing things I didn't want to do, and I hated this.

A high level of resentment built up within me. I lost sight of any natural tendency I had and started to find it hard to make even the simplest of decisions. I no longer knew what I really wanted, so I gave in to other people's power of persuasion again and again.

I would rebel and attempt to reclaim my sense of self. I failed miserably though. I would explode in bursts of rage, shout and scream and try to enforce my opinion.

Afterwards I would feel a heavy sense of guilt on top of the resentment and simmering anger. I would give in and do what the other person wanted with an annoyed reluctance. Or I would start refusing their advice, even if it was clearly useful for me. It was a dysfunctional attempt to reclaim my personal power and individual choice.

Anger was expressed through me every day in many different ways. I didn't recognise this at the time. I just thought it was my personality to be this way.

I was called things like oversensitive, overemotional, stubborn, awkward, uncooperative, unreasonable, and more. I believed there was something wrong with me. Somehow, I was deeply flawed and a victim to circumstance.

Most of my life, from a very young child, I was ill a huge amount of the time. The joy I felt singing and playing was a distant memory which had faded away completely by the time I was a teenager.

I was one of those people who walked around with a dark rain cloud over their head. People used to step back if I was concentrating, because the intense, brooding look on my face scared them. I learnt to paste a fake smile on my face. It all added to a rigid tension in every muscle of my body.

After I had learnt to meditate with the Ascension techniques, I started to release this pent-up anger. This release allowed me space and clarity to see what my triggers were, so I could become more aware. A higher level of awareness gave me the breathing space to begin to choose how I would like to act. This was much nicer than my previous highly reactive anxious state.

With this new state of calm and relaxation, I began to recognise how many ways this old stale angry energy was expressed through me. I would watch as I heard myself speak with a tone of annoyance or irritation in situations that weren't that big of a deal.

Other traits I became aware of were scathing judgement, criticism, intolerance, lack of respect, boredom, fidgeting, restless leg, frustration, agitation, forcefulness, disinterest, and dislike of a huge amount of life. I was often quite horrified as I became aware of these attitudes, that led to behaviour and language I hadn't consciously chosen for.

As I became more aware, I found I still carried out the unconscious behaviour without being able to stop myself. This led to an immense amount of self violence as I judged myself incredibly harshly.

I was reacting in opposition to my values, and this was very distressing. I felt as if I had no control over how I spoke and behaved. This was humiliating and I felt ashamed of who I was.

Over time, as I continued to use the Ascension techniques, these patterns of speaking and behaviour fell away by themselves. The self-violence faded away too as I realised it was unconscious and judging made no difference to the situation.

When you are holding onto anger, you project it out onto the world around you. Your mind continually finds something wrong and blames this external 'thing' or person for the source of your anger.

This isn't true, and therefore the anger is never resolved. Because, even if the external issue is resolved, your mind just looks for something else to blame.

Sometimes this source of blame is directed at ourselves. If we want to get past this pattern, we must redirect our focus within. Not on our mind, but on Silence. With the focus on Silence, we start to release the stored anger and start to experience life with more gentleness and calm.

Gradually, as I learnt to be more gentle with myself, I became more consciously aware, so most of the old, outdated habits stopped.

Anger and all its companions started to be irrelevant. I also realised why previous triggers triggered me and with these discoveries the triggers stopped affecting me to the same degree.

It's so easy to blame others for the way they speak and act towards us. However, if you do this, you keep yourself locked into the pattern of reaction.

This is where surrender helped me the most. To surrender to this moment exactly as it unfolds is incredibly liberating. You cannot do this without becoming more aware, present, and clear minded. As you meditate and clear the decks, you start to see everything is not as it appears.

Hurt people, hurt people. When we surrender, we start to step out of this looping pattern and each interaction becomes purer.

We don't give away our power when we surrender. In fact, in my experience, it's the absolute opposite. When we surrender, we retain our awareness of 'Self' and become empowered.

This change of approach also makes it easier for the other person as well. They can often relax and appear to start being more friendly towards us.

Surrender doesn't always happen in the way we expect it to. It can happen in many different ways. Surrender is definitely not the same as giving in and letting other people rule you.

There was an occasion that totally changed my experience and understanding of anger. Someone was listing everything they decided I had done wrong. I was aware my blood was starting to boil. It was slowly rising within me. However, I became aware of the physical sensation and started to use the Ascension techniques eyes open. They anchored me in a still, silent awareness.

Although it still felt uncomfortable, I was able to watch as if slightly distanced from the other person. Then a realisation struck me out of nowhere - I was only angry because I believed what they said was true. It became comical, as it was now so obvious it was not at all true, it was just their opinion.

I felt a lightness take over and the discomfort reduced little by little and I knew I would remain calm no matter what else they said. I was free in that moment to act how I wanted to, in alignment with my values. I was free to be me.

I still occasionally get angry. It is a rare occurrence these days and never lasts very long. I no longer judge myself for reacting in anger either. I have recognised it is an unconscious reaction that I have no control over.

In these situations, the only way forward is to pause, hit the reset button, watch, and listen. This creates space and the unwanted angry emotion flows through me and leaves. Then I continue with my day from a relaxed, calm state once more.

I hope there comes a day when I no longer react in anger, raise my voice, or speak words that are harsh. But I'm no longer a slave to my anger and I know it is not who I am. This is such a freeing and joyful realisation to learn about myself.

Anger is a learnt habit. What you learn you can unlearn. You just need to want to change and find an effective technique to retrain your brain. Ascension is perfect for this!

Surrender nearly always allows me to calm down. I allow the words that are there to be spoken to flow through me. It isn't always pretty as you transition from an intense reactive angry state to a calm and grounded state. You will need to be supremely gentle with yourself, as you surrender and learn to come back to the real 'you'.

You're in there, deep inside, and you're amazing. Don't let anger rule you. You too can be free to be 'you'.

"Change is never painful. Only the resistance
to change is painful."

- Fake Buddha Quote -
(But true nevertheless!)

Chapter 5
Resistance

Resistance is the opposite of surrender. We've all learnt to resist and it's a very strong, long held habit. It's also mostly unconscious. We don't notice we are resisting, until it becomes so intense that discomfort creeps in.

When we notice discomfort or pain, resistance has been in play for a while leading up to the moment we become aware of it. Pain / discomfort is a mechanism which is designed to get our attention. We typically resist the pain which just further intensifies the physical sensation. We get locked into a battle with ourselves. A futile battle, which increases suffering and makes life unbearable.

Nobody wants to suffer. Resistance, however, is the cause of suffering. It's the cause of <u>all</u> suffering.

We usually want to eliminate something or someone who we believe is causing our suffering. We think if we remove this perceived cause, suffering will end. It may even cease for a while. However, because resistance is the cause of suffering, removing the person, thing or event will not make us happy.

For a start, the judgement towards the offending person, thing, or event, results in us thinking incessantly about it. Suffering continues and thinking is repetitive in a futile attempt to find a solution.

Have you noticed, that if you walk away from someone or something, you come across another person who acts in the same way, or another similar situation arises to replace the one you left?

The resistance happens within us. Changing the external world changes nothing. Suffering will inevitably arise again, until we remain locked into a perpetual state of mental, emotional, or physical pain.

None of this is necessary. Suffering is not necessary. There is another way.

Identifying all the ways we resist is one of the ways we can change this dysfunctional, seemingly never-ending pattern of suffering.

In the recognition of resistance, we become more aware. Noticing, and doing nothing but observing where in our body we feel the resistance, is a useful first step to relaxing and letting the resistance go.

My experience of doing this has meant that I have become much more practised at surrendering.

Every time I notice I'm resisting, or I notice tension in my body, repetitive thinking or an emotion which increases in intensity, I stop... pause... and pay attention.

We cannot think our way out of resistance and suffering. Well, I can't anyway! I know, because I've tried many times, and recognised this just increases the pressure and suffering gets more debilitating.

Thinking is, in my experience, part of the problem. If we think about anything we don't like or want to get rid of, we just keep ourselves anchored to it. Forever.

Thinking locks us into conclusions which are limiting and clouds our awareness. The solution could be right in front of us, and we miss it. We miss it because we see what we think we will see. Thinking can be synonymous with resistance and suffering. Said another way:

Thinking = Resistance = Suffering.

I invite you to explore the validity or falsehood of this statement. Don't write it off until you've explored what happens when thinking slows down and stops.

What is it like to be still now?

A still, quiet mind is incredibly alive, peaceful, and enjoyable to experience. Intuition kicks in and we are free to act and speak from a universal truth. Every word, feeling and action is pure, kind and serves the greatest good for all.

Resistance causes suffering.

Surrender ... and suffering ceases.

Surrender and the mind stills by itself. Surrender and the experience of everything feels gentle and easy.

Whereas resistance distorts everything we see, hear, smell, taste, touch, feel and experience.

Until you strip away all resistance, you will have no idea how easy and enjoyable everything can be. Although, you can start to gain an experience of gentleness when you begin surrendering. Life gets easier just by surrendering some of what you are resisting. It takes the pressure off and allows more fluidity into your life.

It's an alien concept which bears no relation to reality as we know it. Because we've only known ourselves, our bodies, our relationships, and our world through the distortion of resistance.

It's not real.

However, as long as we continue to unconsciously resist, this is how we will experience everything.

I don't know about you, but I want to experience everything free of resistance. I want the pure, clear, unadulterated experience of life.

I want gentleness, kindness, honesty, and freedom. I want to be happy and dance through life with love lighting the way. I want to be fulfilled in every moment, to live a life full of purpose and connection.

I want this with all my heart, with every fibre of my being. I will continue to explore and pay attention, so I can uncover what _is_ possible.

I want to know what delights are hidden underneath the wrapping of resistance.

I'm going to keep exploring what life is like as I surrender again and again.

I'm going to go with the flow of the river of life. Are you with me?

"Self-care is not selfish or self-indulgent.
We cannot nurture others from a dry well.

We need to take care of our own needs first, so
that we can give from our surplus, our abundance.

When we nurture others from a place of fullness,
we feel renewed instead of taken advantage of."

- Jennifer Louden -

Chapter 6
Feeling Safe

I used to feel anxious all the time. I didn't know why, it's just the way I was. I fully identified with the feeling. It defined me. I felt helpless and had no way to be anything other than that.

I didn't know this at the time, but with the benefit of hindsight, I now realise I was simply afraid. It was a state of being. There wasn't necessarily anything in front of me which was dangerous, in the moment I felt anxious. It just was the way it was. I couldn't change it.

So many people, events, situations, triggered my anxiety. I was continually bolstering myself to go on with what I had to do in my daily life. I was walking around with a ball of tension in my stomach all the time. It was more intense in certain situations, but it never left me. I didn't feel safe in any situation, or with any other person. Only when I was on my own could I relax and be myself. It was a very lonely experience.

I wanted to be around other people. I liked to talk and share. I just couldn't let go and relax whilst I was with them. I had to keep the mask on to keep myself protected. Keeping the mask on was very tiring which added to the anxiety and kept it in place.

When I fell in love and married a wonderful man, I was more relaxed with him than anyone else. But still not completely.

Later on, we had two beautiful children who made my life feel complete. I felt safe with them, and it brought out my protective streak. I started to step out beyond what felt comfortable in order to look after them. Only to a certain degree though.

I was so stressed and anxious I didn't look after them as well as I would have liked. Other parents pushed me around, and I was compelled to comply because my fear held me back.

When one of my children was being treated unfairly, there was the odd occasion, when I overcame my fear and acted out of love to say no to the unkind behaviour.

It wasn't easy though, and afterwards I would feel exhausted and over emotional. Fatigue and intense emotion, I've discovered, is a sure sign of feeling unsafe.

Even when my children had friends over for a play date, I didn't feel safe. I didn't identify it at the time. I just knew I was uncomfortable for as long as they were in our house. It was a relief when their parents picked them up and I could relax a little.

I would still be in a state of tension and stress until I got my children in bed and could retreat to the lounge and be by myself. I found I needed a good two hours to wind down enough to be able to go to sleep.

Why was this? Why was I so afraid to the degree that even small children felt like a threat?

I have no idea. I did realise at some point though, that it didn't matter if I didn't know why.

It was a learnt habit, which had gradually built in me throughout my childhood. It was lovely when I recognised it wasn't who I am. When I saw it was merely a learnt response, a defence mechanism built to keep me safe.

Ironic really. The barriers I constructed to keep myself safe, were the very thing which made me feel unsafe.

The good news in all of this is, I started to see the futility in the defensive patterns. It became obvious it was no longer serving me to keep these patterns in place.

Really it was very simple to deconstruct this defence system. All I had to do was notice it and acknowledge it.

Any attempt to get rid of the barriers held them firmly in place. It wasn't something I could force or contrive to do. It was more like an undoing. I started to pay attention and simply notice what it 'felt' like. Where in my body was I feeling fear or anxiety? My body knew how to let it go. I just had to observe the associated physical sensation without trying to change anything about it.

It's easier said than done when the habit is a strong one, because we don't always recognise we are resisting it.

One thing which made a big difference for me was setting up my life to be congruent with peace. There were so many aspects in my home, my relationships and my life which were not functional. I realised I had put up with so many factors which didn't sit right with me.

I was so lost in the story of it all, I hadn't noticed how dysfunctional many aspects were. As my meditation practice released the stress stored in my nervous system, everything became clearer.

Little bit by little bit I made small changes, which started to make a big difference. I learnt to say no. I stopped saying sorry when I'd done nothing wrong. I learnt to stand my ground without being so fierce. I also learnt to trust myself, to follow my intuition and do what felt congruent with my core values.

If you feel unsafe, you are unlikely to surrender. Your defence mechanism will keep you on high alert and fight any attempt to change your approach.

First you must acknowledge how you feel. Not to be right about something, but to simply be with what you feel right now. And explore. What is it like as an experience? Where do you feel it? What happens when you watch the physical sensation with no agenda, commentary or even an opinion?

Don't answer these questions from the mind. Let go of all dialogue about the physical sensation and give it 100% of your attention ... And watch.

Be here, now, and watch.

Your body comes alive when you watch it with all of your attention. It thrives and heals very effectively.

It's not like I began to feel safe either. Rather, I simply stopped feeling unsafe. I got to know my body more intimately. I became present in my body.

Then... my body could get on with its job of maintaining and healing itself.

The unsafe feeling had been derived from a thought pattern. When I stopped paying so much attention to the thought pattern, it faded away.

It's really simple. There's nothing to do. Just pay attention and observe the patterns and they fall away by themselves.

There are so many subtle ways we display fear and anxiety. If we feel stressed in any way, shape or form, there is fear lurking beneath the surface. If we are controlling about anything, fear is running the show. If there is anger within you, fear is behind it.

It's good to identify all the ways fear presents in your life. You never need to try to feel unafraid. Embrace it, and explore the experience, the physical sensations, so you can better understand yourself.

Again, not by thinking about it. Thinking just loops in circles and maintains the fear. Come back to this moment and notice what you are aware of with all your senses. This allows you to step out of your thought created reality and into the now. Into love.

Paying attention purifies our experience, keeping it simple and bite sized.

Being present in the body, means our words and actions come from a place of love and acceptance. We can be gentle and kind, to ourselves, as well as to everyone else.

Love is an inner state of being, a quiet space deep within.

Love is the antidote to fear.

Love will allow you to be you. Fully. Unreservedly. Unapologetically.

Love is the safest space to be. And … you are love.

When you recognise this as a direct experience, surrender happens automatically.

Once upon a time, there was a wise Zen master. People travelled from far away to seek his help. In return, he would teach them and show them the way to enlightenment.

On this particular day, a scholar came to visit the master for advice. "I have come to ask you to teach me about Zen," the scholar said.

Soon, it became obvious that the scholar was full of his own opinions and knowledge. He interrupted the master repeatedly with his own stories and failed to listen to what the master had to say. The master calmly suggested that they should have tea.

So the master poured his guest a cup. The cup was filled, yet he kept pouring until the cup overflowed onto the table, onto the floor, and finally onto the scholar's robes. The scholar cried "Stop! The cup is full already. Can't you see?"

"Exactly," the Zen master replied with a smile. "You are like this cup — so full of ideas that nothing more will fit in. Come back to me with an empty cup."

- Zen Proverb -

Chapter 7
Empty Your Cup

I used to have an answer for almost everything. If I thought I was right about something, I wouldn't let it go until I proved it. Of course, proof can be subjective, but I never saw it that way. The answer would be blurted out before I had time to take in all the parameters. Then I had to stick to my answer for fear of looking stupid.

Nobody else cares if we mess up. Only we do. I cared massively, and never wanted to fail or get something wrong. I held onto my version of truth and would try to persuade others I was right. Only those close to me though. If I met a dominating person, I would often be swayed by their opinion. I would agree before I realised it was not in alignment with my values or natural impulses.

My cup was so full of what I thought was correct, there was no room left for new realisations ... or intuition.

I've since learnt that failing and not having an answer is a blessing in disguise. When we fail, or don't have the answer, we can stop for a moment to assess the situation. When we create space to process the information, we open up our awareness to other possibilities.

In short, we empty our cup. We let go of what we think we know and look again with fresh eyes. We listen and pay attention with fresh ears. Our awareness widens and we begin to see more, hear more, notice more.

If an expectation isn't met, this is actually a good thing. It takes us out of our programming and presents alternative options we may never have thought of before.

Expectations keep us locked into a limited world view. It doesn't 'feel' right when they're not met. But this feeling is misleading. The feeling is based on a conclusion of what we believe is accurate and true.

Just because it 'feels' true doesn't mean it is true.

If our expectation doesn't happen the way we would like it to happen, it may be that another way is presenting itself.

When we learn to go with what happens and let go of our expectations, we begin to open ourselves up to new opportunities.

If we empty our cup on a daily basis, we can experience life in a much more gentle and easy manner. We are no longer beholden to the past. We can see everything much more clearly.

Solutions we've been struggling to find pop up in the most unexpected ways. Life becomes more enjoyable and exciting. We start to see the world is always working in our favour. We just have to get out of our own way, let go and see what wants to happen.

We only have access to a wider range of possibilities if we empty our cup. Holding on to what we think is true is like wearing blinkers. We are blind to 90% of what the world has to offer. A solution or exciting opportunity can be right in front of us, and we'll miss it because it doesn't match our expectations.

How ridiculous is that?!

We are our own worst enemy. We sabotage ourselves every day, and we often don't even notice.

Empty your cup.

Let go of what you think is true, or at least assume it is incomplete. This approach will allow you to be open enough to see a gift horse when it comes your way.

Let go of the need to be right. This can be a tough one to let go of. It was for me, and it still trips me up occasionally. However, I'm now willing to let it go as soon as I recognise I'm doing it. It's incredibly liberating and opens me up to gentleness, joy, and alternative possibilities.

It doesn't matter if you spot yourself holding on or needing to be right. It's a good thing. Something to celebrate even. Because once you notice you're holding on, or needing to be right, you can choose again.

You will likely need space to allow the associated feeling to dissipate. Pausing is a useful tool to help you with this process. Breathing through the feeling is helpful too.

Pause, breathe, and pay attention, so you can allow the process to happen. It will happen much more readily if you don't berate yourself for your reaction.

Reactions happen unconsciously. You can't control them. But you can gradually change how you respond by giving yourself the space to act how you consciously choose to. It takes practice and the willingness to hit the reset button and go again. This way you train yourself to activate new, more positive habits.

In time you will act more consciously, and your cup will remain empty, so you are always open to more!

"Not until we are lost
do we begin to find ourselves."

- Henry David Thoreau -

Chapter 8
Innocence and Curiosity

When it comes to practising surrender, innocence and curiosity are very useful.

Innocence is a way of approaching anything in life to create the most effective results.

For me, being innocent is wiping the slate clean each time you approach something you've done before. Even when you're trying something new it can be helpful to engage innocence before you begin. It gives you the best chance at taking everything in and doing a task more smoothly and easily.

Surrender is much easier to do if you are being innocent. You will be more willing to let go if you have no agenda, judgement, or expectations.

Innocence is a wide-open state of fascination and delight. You have no preconceived ideas, so you're less likely to jump to conclusions.

An innocent approach allows you to be more alert and attentive, so you are able see more, hear more and experience the purity of this moment.

Purity is, in my experience, a clear untainted version of reality. There are no parameters or limitations set by the mind in a pure experience. You get to experience what is right in front of you in a much clearer and more gentle way.

A pure experience is soft, light, and enjoyable. There are no judgements or opinions distorting your experience. Distortion leads to pressure and intensity. Purity leads to free-flowing energy, gentleness, and ease.

Everything in life is much more fun, fulfilling and rewarding when you are innocent.

I find curiosity is another approach which allows me to be innocent with life. When I approach this moment with curiosity I'm fully engaged and fascinated to see what I notice. I'm also intrigued to see how things will unfold.

It's like a science experiment. I may have a hypothesis and an idea about how things will turn out. But I'm willing to explore, ask questions and investigate to observe what appears to be true.

I used to jump to conclusions and run with them as if they were the only answer. Now I observe and continue watching to see if anything changes or more information comes to light.

You see, life is continually changing and opening up in front of us. Curiosity allows me to be fluid and easily change direction if it seems as if things are diverting to a different outcome than I first expected.

Expectations aren't a problem if you let them go as the experience evolves and new options present themselves. There is a natural flow to life and curiosity makes it easier to be flexible when life throws a curve ball.

'When life gives you lemons, make lemonade.' I love this saying. Because sometimes we judge what happens to be bad or wrong. However, if we get curious about the new occurrence, we open up our creative side. When our creativity is engaged, we can discover solutions and options we wouldn't otherwise become aware of.

I'm a strong believer in there always being a solution. If a solution is required. Sometimes when playing with curiosity you recognise there's nothing wrong and you embrace 'what is' with acceptance and joy. But, if a solution is required, it will become apparent when we're being curious and innocent.

There have been many times in the last ten years when I've resisted what is happening. In the moment I recognised the resistance and got curious, paid full attention to see what else I would notice, the thing I was resisting took on a new light.

If it gets hard, get curious!

Our greatest treasures are hidden in plain sight. Curiosity allows us to unwrap the deceptive layer of resistance to find gold nestled within.

We're always given what we need. Sometimes it's the adversity in our lives which teaches us to surrender. In letting go, we experience everything with a greater level of ease and grace.

Innocence and curiosity make life a much more delightful and fascinating dance!

"Sometimes surrender means giving up trying to understand and becoming comfortable with not knowing."

- Eckhart Tolle -

Chapter 9
Letting it all in

Surrender, allowing and letting go all mean the same thing. However, they all sound as if you have to do something. If you try to surrender, allow, or let go, it often feels like an impossible task. This is because we typically approach the process of surrender from the mind. You cannot surrender if you are thinking about it.

It helps to try a different method. Instead of trying to let go, let everything in. 'It' is actually already 'in' and any attempt to ignore or push anything away is futile.

Keeping things away is the real impossible task. Whatever you do, however hard you try, you will never be able to keep something away from you. Any attempt to do so will increase the intensity, and you will suffer.

Forget about trying to control what is happening and let everything in. Absolutely everything. When you do this, everything becomes gentle and clear.

It's like when you do the spring cleaning in your home. You draw back the curtains, pull up the blinds, open all the windows and doors letting the light and fresh air in.

This process of opening everything up allows the building to be cleansed. The fresh air comes in and replaces the stagnant air making everything smell and feel better. The light floods in and everything is warmed up and revitalised. The light also allows you to see the dirt and mess, making it easier to clean and clear it all away.

Applying the same process to our mind and body is just as cleansing. When we let everything in, we stop resisting automatically. As we stop resisting, everything which is no longer useful naturally dissolves and releases.

Letting everything in brings new energy and vitality to our entire being - mind, body, and soul. Everything feels energised, gentle, and easy. We also discover we are now able to receive so many new gifts and opportunities. When we are open to everything, we have the capacity to recognise what we need comes to us as we need it.

We no longer need to search for solutions to problems. As soon as a challenge arises, the means to solve it is also revealed.

Letting everything in allows a constant flow of energy to power us for living life to the full. There is also a constant flow of opportunities and possibilities to make life easy, fulfilling, and enjoyable.

Energy is no longer used to resist and control, so we have an abundant never-ending supply of energy to use for whatever life brings our way.

The body will soften and relax, coming back into harmony and balance. Health will improve as our body is allowed to heal and maintain itself without any tension getting in the way.

Without the pressure and distortion of resistance, everything feels and operates more easily and efficiently.

We get to experience everything we desire and more.

Everything we previously tried to contrive and control happens naturally and effortlessly, just as nature intended, with purity and joy.

We discover everything we ever wanted is accessible or appears as if by magic. Love is the guiding force which lights the way, and everything feels light and easy.

All the thinking and effort will fall away because it is no longer necessary. We become present.

In this state of presence, it becomes apparent that love is always there, no matter what is said or done by other people.

We can begin to recognise love in everything and everyone. Love is always present. As you let everything in, this eternal truth becomes a direct living reality.

Love is the space in between the words of hate and oppression. When we can see this for ourselves, we naturally focus on the space - the underlying reality of unconditional love. What you focus on grows, so life gets really sweet, exciting, and enjoyable.

All this can be your experience just by letting everything in. Do you believe me?

You'll just have to try it for yourself. Prove me right or prove me wrong!

We are well trained at trying, controlling, and pushing away though, so determination and repetition will be required to retrain a new habit of approach.

You cannot let everything in by willing it to be so. Trial and error, relaxation and alert attention will be useful tools to activate a habit of being open and willing to let it all in.

Until you begin to experience letting everything in directly, it will remain a lovely (or scary) concept, which you never get to explore for yourself.

You may need guidance to put this into practise. If you really want to learn how, you will find a way to do it. When you are ready, the teacher appears.

So, get clear. Does what I've said make sense to you?

Do you want to let everything in and discover how easy and enjoyable life can be?

If your answer is no, just carry on as you are.

However, if the answer is yes, pay attention, ask for guidance, and start practising. The means will open up as you take the first few steps.

"Enlightenment is absolute cooperation
with the inevitable."

- Anthony De Mello -

Chapter 10
Acceptance

I've had a bit of a poor relationship with acceptance over the years. This is because I hadn't understood it in the same way as I understand it now.

To accept, meant I had to put up with something I didn't like or agree with. I didn't want to do this, because I had already been putting up with it and had reached my limit of tolerance.

My life had been a battle between what I wanted, trying to keep everyone else happy and to stay safe and protected. Acceptance was a tough topic for me.

Acceptance, for me, meant I would have to open up to the unknown, and I needed to control my world to stay in my safe bubble.

Yet I wanted things to be different. I wanted to be healthy, happy, and abundant, free to be myself and make a positive impact in the world.

I was lost in my concept of what acceptance meant and this tripped me up and kept me stuck.

In my refusal to accept certain people, situations, and the state of my body, I created an immense amount of pressure and friction in my relationship with myself, everyone, and everything.

It wasn't until I met the Ishayas that I realised there was another way, another meaning which is incredibly freeing and much more enjoyable to experience.

I can't even begin to tell you how much relief I've felt over and over again as my understanding of acceptance changed and the resistance fell away. This process happened gradually as I explored acceptance in every aspect of my life. I had to let go of the concept I had of acceptance, so I could open up to the direct experience.

Now, to accept means to land fully in this moment and pay attention to everything equally. It means to put down the sword and surrender to what is. Just for a moment.

Until I stopped fighting and arguing with reality, I couldn't see the world as it really was. My clarity was clouded, and everything appeared to be against me.

It took a leap of faith to put the sword down when it felt dangerous or compromising to do so.

I was and still can be very stubborn. Stubbornness can be a useful asset, or it can be a massive hindrance. I'm grateful I can now discern the difference, most of the time anyway! I can still be blind-sided on the odd occasion when I'm not fully present.

Acceptance levels the playing field. It can open us up to the big picture, so we have a much greater level of clarity. Intuition becomes refined and our world opens up, softens, and feels much easier to navigate.

How do we actually apply acceptance in our own life?

First, notice what you are aware of within your experience right now.

What thoughts do you notice? Is there any emotion present and what is happening in your body?

Then simply rest and observe without needing to change anything. Let go of all ideas, expectations, judgement, needs, and just watch… and listen…

Acknowledge what is present and let it be just as it is for a moment as you continue to witness whatever you are aware of in your body and the room you are in.

This is acceptance.

In my experience, accepting allows me to be attentive. If I accept what is and let go of what I think is true, I instantly become more aware and willing to look again. By looking again, I find I can explore what is <u>actually</u> happening and observe, enabling everything to re-balance and come back into harmony.

Acceptance alone can release so much tension from our entire system and allow healing to happen. Healing in our physical body, healing in our relationships and healing in our life in general.

This release and softening takes the pressure off and clears our mind, so we see much more clearly.

Once we start accepting, it opens us up to an entirely different perception of everything. When we can accept another person exactly as they are and stop trying to change them, our perception of them changes. We see their pain and efforts to do the right thing, when previously we may have seen rudeness, cruelty, and manipulation.

Acceptance creates the space to speak and act with patience and kindness, even in the face of extreme hostility.

We may even be more authentic.

Acceptance frees up our energy, so we don't feel so tired and bored with life.

Acceptance allows us to be more playful and creative, so solutions can be discovered, seemingly out of nowhere.

Acceptance can help a difficult conversation open up and change direction. Acceptance enables us to listen to the other person, so they feel seen and heard. When a person feels seen and heard they feel accepted. When they feel accepted, they become more willing to listen to us in return.

When we accept people, they in turn accept us. When we accept situations, they open up and more options are presented.

Acceptance is a superpower. But we're so busy trying to get what we want; we forget to communicate and listen. We miss out on so much.

Acceptance is a superpower, let's use it and make our lives easier.

"Those who flow as life flows
know they need no other force."

- Lao Tzu -

Chapter 11
Power vs Force

I used to mistake force for power. I now know they're not the same thing at all.

Using force is like operating with the handbrake partially applied. It's approaching life as if we're not going to be supported in our desires.

Forcefulness happens when we argue with reality and try to make what we believe should happen, happen. Even when every sign is redirecting us towards another path, another opportunity. We ignore them all and keep going, trying to make reality align with our expectations.

Not only is this a very painful way to live our life, it's also highly ineffective. It uses an immense amount of energy to force our will on another person or situation. It's also completely unnecessary.

Nothing worthwhile in life needs to be forced. The Universe is trying to support us in our desires and actually has a much clearer idea of how to fulfil them.

We don't need to be forceful. Instead, pay attention and see where the energy wants to flow. Pay attention and notice… What wants to happen?

When we pay attention, we relax, become focused and gain more clarity. Then we are able to recognise our true power come to light.

Congruency happens. We align with our highest desire and action comes through us. Now we're empowered from a very pure place of presence.

When we're aligned with our highest desire, every part of us is going in the same direction. With everything heading the same way, we harness an immense, yet gentle, power which is grounded and harmonious.

We can achieve so much more with much less effort this way. Yielding force can gather many resources around us, all working in our favour.

We free up so much energy when we stop forcing what clearly does not want to happen. This energy works with us, empowering us to act in accordance with the greatest force for good.

Every action carried out in alignment with what wants to happen serves all of humanity. Which includes you.

Sometimes we have to get out of our own way so we can allow events to unfold naturally.

We don't have to give up our desires. However, we will need to be more flexible. It may serve to surrender our immediate wish, so we can free things up to move in a different direction.

Most of us have a strong idea about how things should play out. We force, push and strain against unfolding events until we become exhausted, frustrated, and angry.

We rest, then go again with the same forceful approach.

We are often shocked and annoyed that our expectations still go unfulfilled.

It's crazy really. We keep doing the same thing, and yet expect different results. There's a quote by Henry Ford which illustrates this beautifully.

"If you always do what you've always done, you'll always get what you've always got!"

It says it all really. I love quotes like this. They bring a lot of wisdom and clarity to us.

It seems so obvious once you see it. Yet I used to repeatedly do the same thing over and over and expect different results. I can laugh at myself now, but it used to be a very painful experience.

If something isn't happening in the way you expect, stop for a moment ... Pay attention ... Let go of every expectation and observe for a while.

What wants to happen?

Let everything come into alignment, and work with what you have available to you right now. Let power arise within you and give you what you need to get the job done.

The greatest power may be surrender.

Surrender to what is.

Fear not though... Surrender empowers us and directs us to the course of action which fulfils us so completely, we don't even care whether our initial desire comes to pass or not.

Power is much more effective than force.

It's much more gentle and enjoyable too!

"The most important thing in communication
is to hear what isn't being said."

- Peter Drucker -

Chapter 12
Battle of Wills

Most people these days aren't listening to each other. They're not interested in the opinion or desire of other people, they're just out for themselves.

Even as a people pleaser this was true for me as well. It didn't appear that way though, because I was always doing things to keep those around me happy. However, I was motivated by my own personal agenda every single time. It was a shock when I discovered this!

I had unconsciously learnt to make people happy to keep myself safe. I also wanted to be liked, to be welcomed into the group. Essentially to be loved and accepted.

I began to realise that when I was doing things for other people, I was really doing it for my own personal agenda. This was initially hard to accept because it felt like I was doing something wrong.

I knew I was a good person deep down, and I genuinely wanted to help people. But, so often, fear of rejection, or fear of being harmed, got in the way of my natural desire to help people.

Always doing things for other people also built up a huge amount of resentment. I felt obligated to help some people and it seemed like nobody valued me or cared about what I wanted.

Time and time again, I would find myself in a battle of wills with another person. The only alternative appeared to be to give in and compromise my desires and values.

I didn't know how to ask for what I wanted. Often, I didn't even know what I truly wanted, but had gone for something and been opposed.

Stubborn or aggressive opposition would trigger me to fight back and try to enforce my will. It never went well.

Sometimes I would win and sometimes I would lose. However, it became apparent that even if I won, I still lost. Someone else suffered and that never sat well with me. I hate to see people suffering or doing without.

This didn't stop me though. I appeared to be compelled to assert my own will if someone opposed me. It was a red rag to a bull, and I could be very fierce when I felt threatened or disrespected.

Interactions, when both people insist on their way being the only way, always end in suffering. People stop listening to each other and become dominating or manipulative. They shout, or cry, or become aloof. Anything to get their own way.

This is a very unpleasant way to live. We all just want to be respected and valued. We have natural tendencies we want to follow. More often than not, these tendencies become distorted.

How do we fulfil our own natural desires without getting into a battle of wills with other people?

The first, very easy step, I've learnt to do is to listen. Listen to understand, not just to reply, or state my own opinion, or wish. I began listening so fully, I became aware of more than just the words being spoken.

You can listen for what is not being said. Notice body language. Explore the hidden messages.

As you pay attention, see if you can discern the other persons original intention for their communication beyond the words they use.

You will find as you listen, you start to uncover so much more. You may become aware of the other persons emotional state, start to recognise their true intent, or think of a question to gain more clarity.

You also become more present.

Being present takes the neediness out of the interaction. You start to get curious and open to a more heartfelt connection with the other person. Your own agenda falls away and you become more willing to work with the other person for a mutually beneficial outcome.

It's possible for everyone to have what they want. However, sometimes we think we want something, when in truth we don't. If we listen and pay attention, it starts to alter how we perceive the situation. Some desires can fall away in an instance as we become more present.

Often what we perceive we want, is just to validate us or make us feel better. When we listen with 100% of our attention to what another person says, we become more present, and we find there's nothing to prove.

Doing things to make ourselves feel better, pale into insignificance compared to how we feel when we are fully present.

Listening 100% is a really easy way to become present, to change the dynamic of a conversation and open up to a more friendly, respectful communication.

To listen with all of our attention, is a good way to surrender to the greatest force for good. To let the most beneficial outcome happen for us _and_ for the other person.

We don't need to force our will on another, to fulfil all our desires and live a happy life.

Surrender is much more enjoyable. It's also an effective way to fulfil every natural desire and relate well with our friends, work colleagues and even our family!

Surrender your will to the greater will, and you will live a happy and fulfilling life.

The 'Will of God', as it's sometimes called, is not separate from you. Separation is an illusion. We're not surrendering to another being, we're surrendering to love. Unconditional love.

The 'Will of God', therefore, could also be called the 'Will of Love'.

Are you willing to surrender to love? To let love guide you and direct your life?

This is what surrender means to me. To let the purest, most loving force in the Universe show me the way.

There's no battle of wills then. Just a smooth easy ride through life, connecting with others and benefiting from humanities diverse skill set.

Teamwork makes life easier and more effective. Valuing what everyone has to offer. Letting go of the need to be right, so love can light the way forward.

We can step away from a 'me or you' world and create a 'me and you' community.

Sounds good to me!

"You have peace, the old woman said,
when you make it with yourself."

- Mitch Albom -

Chapter 13
School of Gentleness

Are you gentle with yourself?

The answer is likely to be no, or certainly not all of the time.

We are often our own worst enemy. I know I was really tough on myself. I used to be a perfectionist, and this is a rigid way to approach life. I wasn't just needing perfection in myself, I needed it in the world around me too. There's a very thin line between perfectionism and OCD (obsessive, compulsive disorder).

I used to feel it was a noble trait to want perfection in everything I did. But what is perfect? It is subjective, and often unattainable, so you feel like a failure.

It certainly isn't a gentle way to live your life. In my own experience, as I learnt to relax and calm my mind, I started to see it was incredibly self-violent.

It was quite a challenge to let go of the need for perfection. I realised I would need to cultivate a new habit, a new focus, so I could learn how to approach myself and my life in a more gentle manner.

I've always found that a light-hearted, yet structured approach is the most effective way to change my habits and activate new ones. So, I decided to attend a 'School of Gentleness', where all the lessons are directed at becoming more soft and gentle in everything I do.

Creating the title 'School of Gentleness' amused me and allowed me to be more playful as I systematically made changes to become more gentle.

One of the first lessons I chose was to stop saying 'sorry' when I hadn't done anything wrong. It's a very British trait which is quite tricky to surrender.

When I started this lesson, it was more about noticing that I was saying sorry and recognising it wasn't necessary to apologise. In this exploration I realised I was apologising for being myself, rather than for anything I had done. I felt like I was a nuisance and less than everyone else. Quite sad really.

So many people apologise excessively in this way and feel like they are a bother to others. As I continued with the intent to stop saying sorry, I started to feel less worthless. The heavy energy of the word sorry changed as I stopped identifying with it. I also became more aware of the habit of saying sorry, which gradually released me from the automatic expression of the word.

A choice opened up and over time I stopped saying sorry for no reason. Obviously if I did something like tread on someone's toe by accident, I would still say sorry.

This brought a lot of gentleness into my experience. It was also empowering as I started to stand in my truth and realise, I was worth something.

Another lesson I explored was to move more slowly and consciously. My movements were often rushed, tense and forced. It was quite funny really. I noticed I half ran from one room to another or to go to my car. I wasn't late, so it was entirely unnecessary. I have no idea why I did it. I just wasn't present and seemed to always want to be at my destination as fast as possible.

I was rarely, if ever, where my body was and that caused a lot of friction and pressure on my system.

Again, I started by simply noticing the habit. I discovered that I slowed down immediately without even trying to. My movement became more fluid and graceful. I also stopped getting so many dizzy spells and bumping into the doorway or furniture.

With more gentleness in the movement of my body I became more alert and able to react quickly if something unexpected suddenly happened.

I also felt much calmer and more centred as my body softened and relaxed.

Lesson three was wrapped around blame and shame. I first played with this at my children's school PTA meetings. There was an environment of blame which was harsh. Everyone was on the defensive and ready to attack each other at any moment.

I took over as the Chairperson and simply started to take responsibility for all the apparent mistakes. It took the pressure off everyone, and they immediately relaxed and quite quickly the blame culture fell away.

It was easy for me to change in this area of my life. However, there was still a blame pattern in my family environment. In this case it was much harder to change the habit. I felt judged and the dynamic was much more well developed.

What I began to realise though was, blame was not necessary at all. Nobody was to blame; we were all doing our best.

I wasn't able to take responsibility so readily, but it didn't matter. Just in starting to tell my family it was nobody's fault, allowed a more open and willing dynamic to develop. There is still an element of blame in my family, but I'm much more aware of how it plays out.

As compassion has grown within me, it has provided space and gentleness, so blame is identified and talked about without pointing the finger.

Realising I wasn't to blame was the most important aspect in the exploration of this lesson. As I stopped feeling like I was in the wrong, my defence mechanism relaxed and I let go of my forceful, sometimes aggressive, way of communicating. As blame fell away in my own experience, shame swiftly followed, and gentleness naturally replaced them both.

Gentleness is a natural state of being, so ultimately all we need to do is recognise the patterns of behaviour which aren't useful.

When we can simply be ourselves, with no apology, no blame, no judgement, gentleness naturally arises in our experience.

The invitation for you, the reader, is to take a look at these areas of concern in your own lives. Explore how you can bring more gentleness into your own experience. Notice the self-violent patterns which can be very subtle.

How can you make little changes to let go of your defence mechanism?

It's all based on judgement. Judgement is just an idea or conclusion you came to. Don't let any idea or past conclusion run your life. Nothing is set in stone. Become more aware and allow gentleness to grow and develop in every area of your life. Attend your own 'School of Gentleness' and discover how gentle life can be when we stop apologising, blaming, shaming, and judging ourselves. When we stop doing it to ourselves, we naturally stop doing it to others too.

You've never done anything wrong. The past can't be changed, so leave it alone and live in the present moment. Let gentleness arise in you and direct your life.

Gentleness is important if you want peace and happiness, and even freedom as well. Surrender your self-violence, it serves no purpose. Attend your own 'School of Gentleness', re-align with nature and simply be yourself.

"Always remember,
your focus determines your reality."

- George Lucas -

Chapter 14
Clarity and Focus

Clarity only comes through surrender in my experience. The mechanism of surrender stills the mind and allows you to see more clearly.

The alternative is a busy mind which goes round in circles, with thinking that is scattered and confused. It's difficult to make decisions when the mind is busy and going in multiple directions continually.

In order to still the mind we need only pay attention without agenda or opinion. This is easier said than done because chaotic thinking is a strong and well-established habit. We tend to refer to the mind to check how we are doing, so we don't realise we're actually still lost in thinking.

Focus can be harnessed to gain clarity when we want to make effective and useful decisions in our everyday life.

One-pointed focus is a power tool. It allows every part of us to go in the same direction. This unified approach of focusing activates a higher state of alert awareness.

Space is also created to enable wisdom to arise in our conscious awareness, lighting the way forward to the best possible outcome.

Focus is much more effective when we surrender. The mind's scattered approach and limited capacity to find a good solution leads us down many a rabbit hole. We think we have a great idea, but putting it into practice often goes awry. Our best laid plans often don't pan out, because we don't have the capacity to see all the parameters or the focus to drive it to a successful conclusion.

Surrender allows us access to focus. In surrendering, the mind stills and all the confusion and chaos dissolves. With the space to see and operate more coherently everything lines up to one point of focus and we gain absolute clarity. It's a very enjoyable and peaceful experience and also incredibly fulfilling to become focused on only one thing at a time.

The easy way to facilitate a one-pointed focus is to surrender everything we believe to be true. As we let go of our ideas and beliefs, we gain access to so much more.

The past no longer governs our clarity, and we are free to see everything in its purity. Clarity comes through us when we forget to control and open up to what this moment has to offer.

If you want to make the most useful and productive decisions, try wiping the state clean, and pretend you don't know anything for a moment. You may just find creative solutions come out of nowhere to fill the space you created.

One way to free yourself up is to brainstorm or mind dump. All you need is a blank piece of paper or blank page on your computer. Then you write your goal or problem or the title of a book for example in the middle of the page.

Then, take three deep breaths with your eyes closed. Open your eyes and write down everything that comes to you, no matter how silly or irrelevant it may appear to be. Don't edit at all. Let every idea come through you and write it down. Everything that occurs to you, even if it seems like it's the opposite of what you think is useful.

Ideas that aren't useful can open us up to ideas and solutions that <u>are</u> useful. You never know what you write will inspire next. What we're try to accomplish with this exercise is to free up our creative flow. When our creative flow is opened up, we can discover some amazing insights we wouldn't have access to with a measured and calculated approach.

I sometimes doodle on these pages while I'm waiting for the ideas to start, or if they dry up. Doodling helps me to access my creative side and takes my mind's attention away from the idea that I don't have anything to say or contribute.

You may have other ways to open up and surrender. Whatever you find which brings you to a place of surrender is great. Don't over think this. Be playful and just give it a go.

Clarity and focus are both natural traits and are easily accessed. If you find you can't access either of them, you are possibly trying too hard. Forcing, as I've said in an earlier chapter, does not produce the best results. Maybe listening to music or taking a walk will allow you to relax enough, so clarity and focus can be accessible.

Explore and see what works best for you.

"Change is the essence of life;
be willing to surrender what you are for
what you could become."

- Reinhold Niebuhr -

Chapter 15
Essence vs Personality

Exploring surrender has opened me up to a new perception of myself and the world. There were personality traits within me which I identified with. I actually thought many of them were just the way I was. Many of these traits have fallen away over the last ten years, so I've realised they were just how I had learnt to be to survive in the world.

For example, I was convinced I was shy and introverted. I had been shy for as long as I could remember and was happier in my own company. A loner, yet I craved social interaction. I was never relaxed around others and often tried too hard to fit in. I wasn't comfortable in my own skin.

I was also angry all the time, when I was younger, easily triggered, especially by family members. When I left primary school, I was overwhelmed by the bigger environment of secondary school and became even more shy. I began internalising my anger, so I would be more acceptable to others.

I also thought I was afraid of public speaking. But really, I had just been humiliated and knocked down so many times I became tongue tied in large group situations.

My personality appears to have changed. All the traits that had been a part of me started to fall away This gave the opportunity for my essence to shine through.

The dark, brooding, angry, hard, awkward me gradually changed. I lightened up, became more open and joyful, I also rediscovered a sense of humour I had forgotten existed.

One of the game changers for me was an exercise I did on meditation retreats. It was called the 'Praise Exercise' and involved pairing up, looking into the other persons eyes and praising them for a couple of minutes. Then we would swap places and the person who had received the praise would then praise the other.

I used to hate this exercise, especially as it was often presented as a game. It was not in the least bit fun for me. It felt awkward to give and receive the praise and it was uncomfortable to look directly into a complete stranger's eyes whilst doing the exercise. I dreaded it and felt a huge amount of relief when it was over.

Yet this exercise totally transformed me, from an awkward person, into one who was relaxed and at home giving and receiving praise.

One thing was always pointed out to us during this exercise. The things people say to us as praise are often similar and in contradiction to how we see ourselves.

I thought I was hard, dark, serious, ugly, useless as a parent and also stupid. When I repeatedly heard that people saw me as soft, gentle, intelligent, beautiful, a great mum, light and joyful I was shocked.

What makes this exercise powerful and transformational is that it counteracts the negative chatter in our mind. Looking directly into someone's eyes connects you with the truth of what they say to you. You can't shrink away from it, and you feel the honesty in the other person's voice. Even if your mind thinks they're lying!

I think this exercise literally melted my belief system and allowed me to detach from my negative chatter. As awkward as it used to make me feel, it made a dramatic difference. The uncomfortable feeling was probably the negative pattern burning up.

The experience of taking part in this exercise overrode the unconscious thinking patterns and made me realise, beyond a concept, that who I thought I was simply wasn't real.

My true essence flourished by doing this exercise. I let go of my idea of who I thought I was and started to feel my authentic self grow within me.

It was undeniable. Direct experience trumps our theoretical beliefs every day of the week. The Ascension techniques released the thought patterns and pent-up emotion, so I was more able to connect back to my own heart and true self.

For me, there is a big difference between our personality traits and our essence. One is a learnt habit; the other is our authentic self.

I'm immensely grateful to uncover this difference and begin to be myself, free of all belief and past behaviour. I never thought I would feel confident and comfortable to be myself in all situations. Previous traits are triggered occasionally, but I see them quite quickly these days.

We rely on our minds to tell us what is possible, and it's not an accurate representation of who we really are.

Stop listening to the voice in your head. You don't have to argue with it, just develop a healthy degree of scepticism, so you can start to let go of everything you think you are.

When you let go of who you think you are, you start to connect deep within to the truth, so your essence can begin to blossom from the inside out.

This ability to surrender our limited beliefs about ourselves purifies us. We can start to re-familiarise ourselves with our natural essence and live life without limitation.

It can feel scary to surrender the idea of who we think we are. But, on the other side of this fear, is a freedom that knows no bounds.

I consider myself lucky. My determination and a desire to change has allowed me to surrender enough, to begin to see what is possible beyond the false boundaries of the individual self.

In the past, I didn't trust myself. However, the direct experience of my real essence has shown me how false my ideas and beliefs are. I now trust in the process and happily surrender everything back to the Universe. I'm fascinated to watch myself grow into a more pure, clear expression of who I truly am.

The mind may be afraid because it doesn't understand what is happening. It can't understand. It never will.

I invite you to surrender who you think you are. It's a wild ride, but it's also a lot of fun!

"Authenticity is the alignment of head, mouth, heart, and feet - thinking, saying, feeling, and doing the same thing - consistently.

This builds trust, and followers love leaders they can trust."

- Lance Secretan -

Chapter 16
Authenticity

All my life I had been trying so hard to fit in, to be liked and do my best. I didn't even consider the option to simply be myself. I had no idea I wasn't being myself. I was so busy trying to survive and do the right thing, there was no room left to explore who I was.

When I hit rock bottom, as painful as it felt, it did open up a doorway to do things differently. I started to question the status quo and investigate other options.

It appears that the desire to get answers is an effective tool, especially if it is one-pointed. I'm always amazed by the change of events, with new options opening up, when you are 100% engaged in one direction.

When I started exploring these new avenues of possibility, a strong desire for the truth arose within me.

I just wanted the truth, I didn't care how it looked, as long as it was the absolute truth. The truth for me is a natural thing. Life is much easier than it often appears to be.

When we're trying to be someone who fits in and is liked, we lose sight of who we truly are. This is a shame. The world needs us to be ourselves. We aren't robots, we weren't designed to follow orders. We were designed to be free and open to explore without limitation.

When I was denying my natural impulses and trying to do the right thing, I was incredibly anxious and angry all the time. It's not natural to force ourselves to fit into a box to keep other people happy.

It is not natural and it's not necessary. It is not even really what the other person wants. It may be what they think they want. Everything in place, neat and tidy, following the arbitrary roles we inherit from previous generations. But it really isn't.

We often don't even know why the rules we must follow are imposed upon us.

The thinking mind is very rigid. It doesn't allow for changes in the landscape. Flexibility is not a possibility when we refer to the mind's ideas and beliefs. Trying to follow our minds governing rule leads us down many a blind alley. It also stops us from being ourselves.

You see, the mind is just a collection of thoughts. It's not who we are. Thoughts are just conclusions. In a changing world, thoughts are mostly, if not always, out of date.

We don't need to hold on to thoughts or identify with them. We don't have to stay the same in all situations. Life is fluid and ever changing, so it behoves us to be fluid to navigate the world we live in.

I gradually learnt how to be myself. It surprisingly requires no effort, just a little curiosity and willingness to pay attention and see what wants to happen. There's a natural movement of energy which flows through us and enlivens us. You could call it passion. We are meant to be passionate, excited and ready to follow our hearts.

Being authentic doesn't look any particular way. The natural path forward is ever changing. Simply being, allows us to remain open and see much more clearly, the route which leads to happy conclusions. For us and those around us.

The idea that we must be a certain way can kill our natural desires. Even the idea that we are a certain way can hinder our natural impulses.

Labels can be so limiting. Useful to a degree, but only if we are flexible enough to see beyond them.

Being authentic is a moment-by-moment evolution. Our natural state is one of surrender, of wonder and awe. This allows us to be open to the joy in life. It allows us to be ready for anything. Not because we are prepared, but because we are powerful beings of light who are capable of anything. We don't know what is possible until we give it a go.

Simply being myself has allowed me to be resourceful and playful. I'm no longer squashed by life's ups and downs. The reactive state I used to live in has fallen away. Authenticity creates space to act in accordance with my core values of honesty and kindness.

Authenticity feels gentle and serene. There's absolutely no pressure, no intensity. Everything that comes my way becomes a gift to utilise for the most amazing results.

The mundane comes alive and vibrant. The little things in life are so much more rewarding. The gentleness of being myself means I have so much more energy for doing what I love. I'm willing to go for what I desire, with the flexibility to change course if circumstances dictate.

Being authentic is a superpower. It's crazy that it's so difficult for us to simply be true to ourselves.

Living in a world which discourages our natural tendencies is not healthy for us. It is vitally important that we come back to our own heart and discover who we really are.

It's so easy to surrender when we're at one with our self, at one with the world. Authenticity is a continually surrendered state of being. It requires no effort. All the signs point us back to centre, to who we really are.

If there's a brick wall in your way, don't try to scale it. Look for other options, be open to another way. All of life is geared to support us. The authenticity of being myself, lights up the way forward. It's like I'm empowered to do whatever wants to be done when I'm true to myself.

Imagine a world where everyone is being themselves. What would that look like? I think it would be beautiful.

We all have talents the world needs to progress and live in harmony. When we're able to be ourselves we are also able to access our innate skills and creativity.

To be authentic is to be happy. Everyone wants this. Everyone wants to stop trying and be happily in tune with themselves. One thing I discovered on my own path of self-discovery is, if you give to others what you want, you will receive it too.

For me this looks like letting the people around me be themselves. As much as I can do. To let them make their own choices even if it doesn't make sense to me. We're all different we don't have to all do the same thing. Diversity is healthy and the best way to create a happy, prosperous, abundant environment for us all to thrive in.

Fear can hinder us in our bid to be authentic. We can be afraid of so much. But fear only operates in the shadows. The bolder and more courageous we can be, the more we step free of fear and into our true Self.

Focus on what you love, what makes your heart sing. If something doesn't go your way, don't spend any energy trying to change it. Look around you, what else is available, what riches are here for you now. The world will guide us, we don't have to think about the options.

It's so much easier to be open to what else wants to support us, than keep knocking on a closed door. To be authentic means to me to be open, to be relaxed. It frees up energy and is a lot more gentle and fulfilling.

There's a musician called Yungblud (Dominic Harrison) who champions being authentic. He's an inspiration for so many young people. He lives his values and makes no apologies for who he is. Some people hate him, but a growing community love him. The haters don't really know him. They can't or they wouldn't judge him so harshly.

I love his authenticity. I love how he encourages his fans to be themselves no matter what. He has created a community based on love, acceptance, kindness, and creativity. His values align with my own and his music is raw and heartfelt.

Dom sees Yungblud as the community of fans - a unified group of individuals who all support each other. To be part of a community without judgement, where you're encouraged to be yourself is incredibly nurturing and healing.

I love Dom, Yungblud, and the community. I love who Dom is, what he stands for and how willing he is to change the world for the better.

We need more people in the world to be like Yungblud. To follow our hearts and dare to be who we really are. It takes courage, but there's so much joy in doing it.

It's much easier and more fun to be yourself in a community of like-minded individuals.

Look for your tribe, your kind of people who look at the world like you do. Expect the very best and be willing to step outside of your comfort zone.

I'm finding the more I go for what I want and be myself with all my heart, the more the world reflects back to me the truth of who I am.

If people shut you down, look for people who will let you be you. They're out there and they're waiting for you to find them. They need you as much as you need them.

Together we will be authentic and change the world for the better. Light dispels darkness, we just have to turn on the light of authenticity and watch as the shadows disperse.

"The difference between ordinary and extraordinary is that little extra."

- Jimmy Johnson -

Chapter 17
Extra-Ordinary

I always used to find the word extraordinary a bit contradictory. You add the word extra to ordinary and it seems to state the opposite. In recent times, however, I have begun to see the word differently.

The magic is in the ordinary everyday life stuff in my experience. The more we open our eyes and pay attention to the ordinary, the more extraordinary it appears to be.

When you put the word extra in front of ordinary you just make more of the ordinary. There's extra ... more of what is ordinary. Nothing has to change; we can just pay extra attention to what appears ordinary, and it transforms into something special.

I think this is where I used to miss the point, where most of us miss the point. We're so busy looking for something better, we don't see what is here now in all its brilliance. We look, but we don't see. We don't completely connect with what's in front of us.

It's so easy to dismiss things when you don't have a full and complete experience of it. Because we're not fully engaged with our world, we often find it dull or boring. We tune out and don't get to experience the full spectrum of something. We decide we don't like things without giving them a chance.

There appears to be a climate of dislike in the world right now. So many people complain or criticise, and it is demoralising. What you focus on grows, so this society of moaners keep getting more and more to complain about.

I set myself a challenge many years ago. The challenge was to do a complaint fast. Every time I noticed I was complaining I stopped in my tracks and chose to find something to appreciate about it. It was an eye-opening experience. I knew I complained, but I had no idea how much I descended into moaning. It could be so subtle. Complaining was a strong default approach towards so many areas of my life.

It was shocking and made me feel awful about myself. But as I explored and kept going with it, I became more playful and determined to change the tide.

Really it was an exercise in increasing awareness and surrender. Once I got over the horror of how negative I was, I found the challenge liberating.

After a month of playing this game, I was so much more aware of how I spoke and so it became easy to stop and choose again. I felt so much lighter and more relaxed too. Complaining creates a heavy energy and brings more of what we complain about to us.

Complaining is an attitude, a learnt behaviour.

Thankfully!

It's possible to stop and put more focus on what is good and what we want more of in our lives.

Paying attention to the ordinary is such an eye-opening exercise to explore. It's human nature to try to avoid what we don't like or seek out something more exciting.

Wouldn't it be wonderful if we stopped this approach and looked closer at the ordinary life we have? What is our life really like and what is in it?

To pay closer attention to the ordinary is a revolutionary approach. But it's such an important shift to make. Let's make the ordinary extraordinary so our lives can be full and exciting without having to change a thing.

This is also surrender in my eyes. Surrender to what is. You can only explore something once you've accepted it into your experience.

The ordinary can only become extraordinary when we surrender and explore what is here now. You do have to allow something be here, now, in order to examine it more closely.

On closer inspection, pretty much everything looks different to how we expected it to look. There are so many facets to everything, which can only be revealed by taking it in fully.

Let's make our everyday ordinary into extraordinary and live the best life possible... are you with me?!

"Normality is a paved road:
It's comfortable to walk, but no flowers grow."

- Vincent van Gogh -

Chapter 18
Natural vs Normal

There is a distinct difference between what is natural and what is normal. Normal is an overused word in my experience. Normal can often be used to suggest something which one person, or a group of people, think should be happening.

Normal for me means something which is consistently happening. Many things happen in today's society which we classify as normal. But it's only normal because it's been happening for a while and is likely to continue happening. The fact that something regularly happens does not make it necessary, and often it is far from natural.

It seems to be normal for many dysfunctional things to happen. It's normal to resist. It's normal to feel anxious. It's normal to have a complicated, pressure filled life. Lots of things are normal and happen time after time in everyday life.

The time has come for us to start assessing whether these normal everyday, often dysfunctional, things need to keep happening.

We need to take a good look at what we are repetitively doing in our daily lives and question: Is it necessary? Is there a better, more functional way?

Another good question is, what is natural?

Natural for me is what is easy, fluid and feels gentle. It is an approach which intuitively makes sense to us. Not just theoretically, but also practically.

Natural is sustainable. Normal often isn't. Natural requires no effort, or strain, or control. Normal can often take a huge amount of effort, strain and can be very controlling. How many times have you heard someone say, "it's normal", when it feels far from pleasant or functional?

How many times have you heard people say, "we've always done it this way", when you've questioned something which seems counterproductive to you?

How much longer are we going to continue making it okay to say something is normal, or we've always done it this way, so we need to keep doing it?

In my own life, I'm looking at places where I can make my life easier and more simple. I like simple!

Natural for me, makes much more sense than normal. I don't want to keep doing things I've always done if it is unnatural, difficult, unpleasant or uses a lot of energy.

This can be quite a challenge. We are creatures of habit, and it can feel hard to change something if you've been doing it for many years.

But change we must if we want to be happy and healthy.

I find it is easier to change something if I approach it in a playful and creative manner. Small changes can lead to a big difference in our lives.

Natural always requires less effort and little to no thinking. Which makes it sustainable, more simple, and pleasant.

Life can be so easy and enjoyable. In my experience, looking for ways to come back to a more natural approach is a highly effective way to keep life simple, happy, and fluid.

I'm always checking to see what wants to happen. If I have to force something, it's clearly not natural or in my best interests.

Natural is flexible and yet also incredibly powerful. Less effort creates greater results when you are in alignment with your natural state of being.

We all have a different approach to life. What is natural for some is not natural for others. Let's honour each other's choices and allow people to do things in the way which is easiest for them.

Make suggestions for sure, if you see someone is struggling or forcing something which clearly isn't working. But let people figure it out for themselves. What is best for us may not be best for them. We are all capable of coming back into balance and harmony, or discovering what is natural and easy for us.

Sometimes I do something which I know isn't necessary, but it makes me feel safe and eases the pressure on me. I go with the habit rather than try to change it. This makes me relax and the re-balance towards natural happens by itself. I am able to see more clearly when I stop resisting my needs and insecurities.

It's so empowering to be allowed to mess up or follow patterns which give a sense of security. I find I'm able to step out of the pattern, out of my comfort zone, when nobody pushes me, which includes myself!

We will naturally come back into balance and harmony when we relax and allow ourselves the choice. Self violence, which is normal, but definitely not natural will fall away when we stop making our habitual behaviours wrong.

Let's explore with a playful and creative attitude... look at everything we perceive as normal … then ask ourselves: is there an easier, more efficient, or pleasant way?

Keep it simple. Natural will find you, as you start reducing the effort and increasing the curiosity along with the willingness to make it easy.

"This whole world is secretly set up
to benefit you."

- Maharishi Krishnananda Ishaya -

Chapter 19
Split Desire

We all want to be happy and lead a fun and fulfilling life. But desire can be something which trips us up.

Typically, most of us are split when it comes to our desires. We are scattered in our approach, and this dilutes the power of desire.

A split desire causes the difficulty in our lives. Get one-pointed on something, anything, and life gets supremely easy.

Look to see where the split is. For example, 'I want peace, but I want my partner to stop snoring'. Or 'I want peace, but I want my headache to go'.

Drop the second desire and be one-pointed on peace.

A one-pointed focus is much more effective and efficient at delivering our wishes. This is why, as an Ishaya teacher, I ask a question at the beginning of our First Sphere Courses.

The question I ask is: "What is your highest desire?"

It's a powerful question!

Some answer this question easily, whilst others stare at me with a blank look on their face.

Most people have never considered this question for themselves. Hardly anyone has ever been asked it before attending the course.

I think it should be asked in schools, colleges, universities, and the workplace.

We need to know what we want more than anything else. It can be our guiding light, our smooth and easy navigation system.

It also simplifies every part of our life when we know the answer to this question and apply it to every situation in front of us.

What is your highest desire?

If you're willing, answer this question right now. Then write it down and put it in a prominent place where you will see it every day. Preferably first thing in the morning.

Let this question, and the answer, be the foundation for every single day.

My answer to this question is freedom. Freedom to be myself, to live life without limitation and move forward through every moment with ease and grace.

As you can tell from my answer, our highest desire is not objective, it's a state of being.

We may desire a new house, good health or even a loving relationship. However, this is not our highest possible desire. Our highest desire is the state we attain when our objective desires are fulfilled.

For example, if we get a new house we will be happy, with good health we will be peaceful and with a loving relationship we will experience love.

I come back to my highest desire again and again. It holds me steady and clears my mind when life throws me a curve ball.

I also find it useful in the little moments as well. For example, if I notice I'm thinking about a conversation or situation that has already happened and perhaps didn't go the way I would have liked. In the moment I notice I'm thinking about it I ask myself: "Is this prioritising my highest desire of freedom?"

The answer is usually no!

So, I choose again. I shift my focus onto the task at hand and give it my full attention. As I become fully present, I recognise the freedom in this moment which powers me forward with a lightness in my being. If I'm walking it literally lightens my step and brings me joy.

It really helps to have a tool to bring your focus back to this moment. The mind likes to wander and flit from one desire to another. Or, more often than not, it moves from one problem to another.

This wandering mind approach does not keep us on track to our highest desire. Latching onto a problem, conversation, or situation we don't like and want to change keeps our desires from being fulfilled.

With a split desire, we are confusing the Universe, so it cannot deliver our wishes to us. If, for example, you really want something and you're not getting it, you'll find you have a split desire. You want to be happy, but you often aren't happy because you want something you don't currently have. When you don't get the thing you want, it distracts you away from this moment.

Your mind will go over and over how to get what you want, why you're not getting it and many other angles on the same topic. Your focus goes round and round in circles and your desires remain unfulfilled.

This approach is ineffective and keeps you focused in the past or future.

To simplify your approach, you're going to want to come back to the here and now. Not only does it simplify everything to be here and now, it also maintains your focus on the source of your highest desire.

This brings us back to surrender. When we surrender our wants and needs, we open the doorway to fulfilling them.

To keep our focus on our highest desire allows us to surrender the specifics and trust our desires will be fulfilled.

Trust is activated by retraining our focus. It's activated by direct experience. The more we surrender our desires and come back to the here and now, the more opportunities and possibilities arise in our lives.

Our desires get fulfilled in the most unexpected ways and we begin to realise we can let go and trust.

Action is still required, but action with a single point of focus is highly effective. If you're not getting the results you want, pause, pay attention and be alert to whatever you are aware of right now.

Let this moment fill you up and bring you the energy and clarity to move forward in alignment with your highest desire.

You may want to find a tool or technique to retrain your focus. If you do already have an effective tool, seek guidance to help you use it to the greatest effect. Guidance from someone who knows how to practice the technique and apply it well.

Simplicity is usually the key to make any tool or technique most efficient and easy. The practice being enjoyable is a sign that you are heading in the right direction, one which serves you best.

Ascension is the tool I use. Ascension is not just a collection of techniques. Ascension is a teaching of the 'One' and it keeps everything simple and easy.

There are always bumps along the way as the stress releases and life shows you where you're holding on. But guidance helps you navigate the bumps much more quickly, smoothly, and easily.

However, you choose to go forward, let your highest desire light the way and keep your life one-pointed, fun, and easy.

"Love is simply the name for the desire and pursuit of the whole."

- Plato -
The Symposium

Chapter 20
Recognition

We are all creating the life we live. This can be a tough concept to accept if our life isn't going so well. We are not to blame for how our life is being created though. It's not our fault.

The reason we're not to blame is because most people are unconsciously creating. We don't know what is in our unconscious mind, so we have no capacity for choice to redirect the life we are living.

This is so important to understand. For me this takes the self-violence out of the experience. We aren't consciously choosing to suffer if we are suffering. However, we are choosing for it unconsciously.

The only sane course of action, therefore, is to become conscious of all the thoughts and emotions which are ruling our life.

Until we become aware of the thought patterns and thinking governing our perception, we will continue to experience emotions and body sensations through the filters of the mind.

Every thought we've identified with keeps us bound to a distorted, pressure filled experience, which makes life harder than it needs to be.

Recognition is an important part of the process. Until we gain enough space and clarity to recognise these internal thought patterns, we will be subject to experiencing a life matching the content.

For example, if we have worry thoughts about something, we will always be governed by a 'something will go wrong' attitude. With worry thoughts running rampant, the mind and body will be on high alert, and we will feel the pressure building up and up. Fear and a sense of danger runs the show. It is very difficult to function with this pattern running amok.

The first step in changing anything is to investigate, so we can uncover all the factors in play which affect our perception and experience.

Investigation in this context means to pause and pay attention with all our senses and see what we notice.

When you notice something, anything, look again to see what else you may notice. Then continue your investigation and explore again to see what else you become aware of.

We're so used to investigating by referring to the mind's conclusions and beliefs. However, most people rarely get to recognise the mechanism which is unconsciously running their life.

Until you stop and get curious, you are unlikely to uncover the truth behind your suffering. The mind is a tricky thing to extricate yourself from. We are so identified with the unconscious thinking patterns, we don't recognise how attached we are to an automated program of thinking and understanding.

Most of this program of thinking was downloaded into our unconscious mind at a very early age. We didn't consciously choose for it. Basically, whatever was repeated often was downloaded, and essentially, we agreed with it.

Or it could be that a traumatic experience happened, and we downloaded a defence mechanism to attempt to keep us safe from a reoccurrence of the trauma.

Most people in the world today have an underlying belief that they are not good enough, not lovable. It's utter nonsense. But, because we experienced one event or a series of interactions which appeared to devalue us, we came to believe we are worthless.

To go beyond this insidious and false programming, we need to stop listening to our internal dialogue. Why? Because listening to and believing the dialogue reinforces the underlying thought patterns.

We need to create an environment which allows us to stop and observe for a period of time, so we can start to reveal the mechanism of the mind. The mind is simply a collection of thoughts running on repeat. It requires our attention <u>and</u> our agreement to remain in place.

It's actually really easy to change. It is a strong pattern though, a firmly entrenched habit. It therefore requires repetition and persistence to cultivate a new habit.

Patience is useful too.

It takes time to retrain our focus away from the thought patterns. We're pulled back into suffering, and again swim in the thoughts.

We can't find our way out by thinking. Which can be a problem, because it is generally the main tool we use to navigate life.

The trap most people fall into, is one of trying to think their way out of the situation. Thinking is the root cause of the problem, so you can't think your way to freedom.

Instead, we must become quiet and begin watching, listening, and paying attention. Look again and again at what appears to be true with curiosity and innocence.

This approach creates space and allows us to see what is <u>actually</u> true, to discern what is <u>actually</u> happening.

In the recognition of what <u>is</u> happening, of what we <u>are</u> doing, what we <u>are</u> thinking, the pattern starts to dissolve.

Typically, as the patterns dissolve and the stress leaves our nervous system, we get pulled back into thinking.

Stress leaves our nervous system in many ways. The body heals as the stress releases. Healing is an active process. The activity in the body reflects in the mind as thoughts.

Meditation is a tool which is designed to give us an alternative focus, so we get more practised at letting the thoughts come and go.

Each time you use a meditation technique, you calm down your entire system and detach from the thoughts.

With an effective meditation technique, we can also begin to cultivate alertness. A high level of alertness allows us to become more consciously aware of the still silent backdrop of pure conscious awareness.

We are the conscious awareness.

We are that which is aware of the thoughts.

No matter what the content of the thoughts, conscious awareness remains unmoving, unchanging and untouched by any thought. Even the extreme, scary, disturbing thoughts. Even the demoralising and self-deprecating thoughts.

The thoughts themselves have no power. They require our attention and engagement to remain in play.

When we can begin to see the thoughts and let them go, we start to become aware of the awareness, which is aware of the thoughts. The more familiar we become with this awareness, the more we begin to recognise we are the awareness. Pure and unadulterated.

All the thoughts are irrelevant, and thinking is unnecessary.

It doesn't matter if you still think.

Recognition of yourself as the witness of life unfolding, the witness of thoughts, emotions and body sensations sets you free. Free to simply be yourself: Still, Silent Awareness, conscious of everything and attached to none of it.

Recognition is all it takes to become free.

You never need to fight against, force, or change anything.

Freedom lies in recognising who you really are. Disidentifying with who you think you are and coming back into alignment with the still, silent self: aware and at peace. A peace so full, there's no room left for stress, fear, hatred, or suffering.

To recognise who we really are, means to re-cognise our Self. To reconnect with our original factory settings.

To cognise means to know directly. We're simply re-cognising and remembering who we are. Who we truly are, without the mind (bunch of thoughts), telling us who we are.

Recognition is coming back to truth, coming back to love, unconditional love.

Get curious ... pay attention ... so you can re-cognise your Self.

The world changes because we recognise who we are, not because of what we do. Our actions follow our recognition of truth, so recognition of Self, of Stillness/Silence is the foundation for pure action.

Pure action and unedited words can change everything.

This is living a life in surrender, always following the heart and being in alignment with the best possible outcome.

"Awareness is the greatest agent
for change."

- Eckhart Tolle -

Chapter 21
Awareness

Awareness is the one thing which increases our chances of choice. We can't choose effectively when we don't have access to all the factors impacting us in any given moment.

We're always aware of something. But what we're aware of may be distorted by resistance and limited by our perception.

What we perceive is, more often than not, a reduced version of the world dictated by our internal beliefs.

We operate based on what we think and feel is true, valid, and necessary. However, what we think and feel may be missing some essential information.

The more we can raise our level of conscious awareness, the more choice we have and the more accurately we can respond to what is actually happening.

Our awareness is infinite and unbounded. But we are only consciously aware of what we pay attention to.

Typically, most people pay a lot of attention to their thoughts and emotions. Thoughts and emotions cloud our awareness. We often don't get to see the full picture, because we pay attention to what we have learnt to believe is true.

If you imagine looking through the inside tube of a toilet roll and pretend that's all you have access to. It's very limiting, isn't it?

Every belief limits our attention, so we only note that which we are in agreement with. This agreement isn't our choice though. It is a conclusion we came to, often at a very young age, before we were able to discern what was useful for us. Most conclusions are negative and are based on unprocessed experiences.

Repetitive or extreme language, behaviour and situations have taught us we are not good enough and have to adjust our approach and behaviour to remain safe and loved.

It is incredibly freeing and empowering to consciously expand our awareness and refocus our attention away from these conclusions.

Thoughts are just ideas, not essential truths. Emotions are a record of the past, an unprocessed feeling which has a story attached to it.

To purify our experience and come back to a clearer perception of reality, it is helpful to expand our attention from the content of life to include the context.

If you look at how our visual system operates it can help to understand how this is beneficial for us. Eyes see clearly when they have a point of focus with a strong peripheral vision. This allows for a soft, relaxed eye which can function easily and effectively.

It is the same with our awareness.

It's natural to have a point of focus which is directly in front of us in this moment, as well as an expanded awareness of the still, silent space. Said another way, our point of focus is on the content and our peripheral awareness is on the context.

If we can do this, we are present, relaxed and can see the big picture without effort or strain. This expanded state of awareness gives us the best chance of having a choice and feeling calm, happy and excited to be alive.

Awareness is everything. We can only choose for that which we are aware of. We can only see all the factors of a conversation or situation if we are attentive to everything equally.

Expanded awareness is our natural state. We've just learnt to contract our awareness to follow thought and emotion. It's not bad or wrong to do this, we're just doing what we've been taught to do.

As young children we learnt far more from copying the adults and older children, than we did from anything we were told. Unless what we were told was backed up by action and then we took the lesson in. Especially if it was repeated over and over.

Even though we've learnt to remain contracted and identified with our thoughts and emotions, we can still choose again.

To exercise our awareness muscle and engage our fully expanded state is very easy to do. However, just like any muscle which has been in a contracted state for a while it has reduced functional abilities. Therefore, we will need to gently exercise it to regain the full range of movement.

We simply need to retrain our awareness muscle to remain alert and expanded to its full capacity. Surrendering what we think we know, what we think we feel, allows us to expand our awareness.

Paying attention will expand our awareness. If we descend into thinking again, we just need to pause and pay attention again.

Our chances of successfully re-engaging the full range of our awareness are increased if we use a technique to retrain our focus.

Meditation is the most powerful and effective way to do this. The techniques I use are called Ascension Attitudes. These techniques are mechanical and easy to use. Every time you use an Ascension attitude your awareness is expanded, and you become more present. Your attention is directed onto Presence.

Initially it can be fleeting, but after a while, the fleeting experience will stabilise. You will then be able to consciously recognise it and remain present, more fully aware for longer and longer periods of time.

Automatically and systematically, you will release all your thought patterns of belief and start to become more aware. Your mind is purified and clarity increases.

Ascension means to go beyond the mind, beyond the thinking patterns and it works even if you believe this is impossible. As long as you consistently practice the techniques that is.

It's like going to a gym for the mind. Your awareness muscle will only strengthen if you use the techniques every day. One of the things I like about the Ascension Attitudes, is that you can use them eyes open as well as eyes closed. Your attitude literally changes as you continue to practise these techniques.

They also take the effort and strain out of life and bring back a state of simplicity and ease. Life is meant to be lived in full conscious awareness. It's much more enjoyable and peaceful this way.

I encourage you to increase your level of consciousness, so you get to choose a life which is fulfilling, creative, easy, and fun.

Nobody chooses to suffer, but we're so entrenched in our thought created realities, we don't even know what is possible beyond our current state of mind and situation.

Until you're fully aware, you won't ever have access to the full range of all that life has to offer you.

Surrender your limited beliefs. Surrender them, so you can have a pure, clear experience of who you really are and the life you were born to live.

It is helpful to assume you only have part of the picture in any given moment. When you operate as if everything you perceive is incomplete, you are more open to receiving the piece of the puzzle which brings you more clarity.

Reclaim your full awareness. Reclaim your birthright. Don't wait ... do it now!

"Choice implies consciousness - a high degree of consciousness. Without it, you have no choice. Choice begins the moment you disidentify from the mind and its conditioned patterns, the moment you become present."

- Eckhart Tolle -

. . .

"May your choices reflect your hopes, not your fears."

- Nelson Mandela -

Chapter 22
Choice

Choice is so important. We are much happier when we are not forced, much happier when we have variety and options.

Life can be full of choice, open and free. But we don't always get to experience all the possibilities available to us.

Why? Because we have learnt to listen to our mind. We have had experiences which have taught us we don't always have a choice. In some cases, we may never have been given a choice at all.

You see, many people live under the shadow of fear. We batten down the hatches and concoct many plans to make sure we are protected from danger.

This danger could be real. It's always possible, and therefore important, to learn discernment. But the majority of perceived danger is merely an idea created in the mind. We may have learnt this idea of danger from others, or we may have come to our own conclusions.

The mind believes it is a separate entity and wishes to remain alive, so to speak. We have learnt to identify with the thoughts running through our mind, so any type of disagreement with the current line of belief is met with aggression or the strong desire to flee the situation.

We have such strong beliefs, most of which are outdated, no longer relevant and some may never have been true in the first place.

Every belief we hold onto is a limitation, a judgement, which governs our words, feelings, and actions. Even if a belief seems innocuous, it still reduces our capacity for choice.

We only really have a choice when we let go of the past and are free to perceive this moment in its purity. Without a thought or conclusion telling us about what is happening.

The idea that anything is wrong is the most debilitating thought. If we believe this idea in any way, shape, or form we will feel the wrongness in the thing or person which is deemed bad or wrong.

This idea, and associated feeling of bad or wrong, colours our perception, reduces our clarity and is never true.

Yes, someone in your life may behave in a dysfunctional way. But it's important to differentiate between the action and the person carrying out the action. Hate the sin not the sinner.

The original meaning of the word sin is apparently derived from another language. It was originally said to mean to 'miss' or 'forget'. In Spanish sin means without, which also works.

So, what are we missing, forgetting or without?

Presence.

When any dysfunctional or harmful act is carried out, the person doing it is not present. They have forgotten who they are. They are not conscious of their true nature. They are without their full awareness and are subscribed to a belief system.

Every human being does what they think is right or best for them. As long as we have a set of beliefs we subscribe to, we are limited in the choices we have.

We react and act based on our belief system. A belief system is created based on the example set by the adults and older children surrounding us when we were young. How we were treated and what we were asked, or made to do at a young age, shapes our sense of self and values.

Most of us are, the majority of the time, simply following our internal programming. We have no choice. We are subject to the content of our minds. We are prisoners to past circumstances and controlling attitudes.

However, there is always the possibility of a choice. If we learn to stop listening to our thoughts and begin to become consciously aware of our still, silent, Self, we can experience freedom. Choice then becomes available to us, and clarity develops to guide us smoothly through the challenges life presents.

Surrender is the means to be able to choose.

As we surrender all our thoughts, feelings, and actions to a greater will, we go beyond them.

We stop identifying with what we think, say, or do, so we no longer suffer the pain of being out of step with reality.

Reality can be experienced without any filters and the pure experience of life is gentle and graceful.

Choice is a wonderful thing!

Surrender is the pathway to greater choice. Pure unadulterated clarity lights the way to words and actions which uplift and inspire us. We can share this with others and create a world full of peace, love, and joy.

Imagine if we were all free to choose whatever we wanted.

Imagine if nobody had any control over anybody else.

Imagine if we all respected each other's choices and encouraged each other to be ourselves.

Imagine if we worked together utilising everyone's natural abilities and skill sets.

What would the world be like then? I believe this is possible and well within our reach.

All we need to do is show up ... Surrender the things we think we know, so we can choose again, free of the past.

This is a brand-new moment.

Let's choose again.

Be present, be open and free. Surrender the past, listen to, respect, and support each other.

Let's choose for freedom... peace... love... acceptance... kindness... and joy. And... let's do it now.

"The power of a river is harnessed when you go with the flow."

- Maharishi Krishnananada Ishaya -

Chapter 23
Step into the Flow

Life can be easy, or it can be hard.

There is a flow of change which continuously moves through your life. If you go with it, life is easy. However, most people have the tendency to resist the natural flow of events and wind-up suffering.

It needn't be hard. In fact, in my experience, life is designed to be easy. Everything we need can come to us effortlessly, easily, and at the perfect time.

I didn't believe this was true until I started to access a present state awareness and life freed up. I won't be surprised if you don't believe it either.

We need to make some changes if we want to be able to recognise the easy flow state in our lives.

Surrender is the path to ease and grace. When we surrender the control we are so addicted to, we can begin to see it's not actually necessary or useful to tightly control everything.

It's counterproductive even. We stop the flow of good coming our way when we try to control everything. Or we simply miss the good which is flowing our way, because we are only looking for things which match our expectations.

Control can make us feel safe. The sense of order we try to maintain can seem reassuring, but it is also incredibly limiting. When we follow the same criteria for living our life, we remain in an experience which will always bring the same results.

We try and try to change something, and we only manage tiny increments which make little to no difference. Disappointment follows and we remain stuck.

There is another way.

We can loosen up and start to expand our awareness to take in new experiences and opportunities.

We can surrender the control in lots of different ways. Start small and build up. Bite size changes can be more sustainable. If you're more daring, you can make bigger changes immediately.

Whichever option you choose, you'll need to make at least one change to open up to new opportunities. To step into the natural, easy flow through life, you will also need to go with what is occurring in your daily life.

Sometimes we need to take a step back and observe from a neutral place. Let go of any agenda or opinion and take stock of our current circumstances.

Just to simply pause and pay attention can bring a huge amount of clarity and space. Space to see the bigger picture and see what wants to happen.

Going with what wants to happen is a very powerful thing. We are then able to harness the natural flow and allow it to power us onward on the path which is best for us. The path which brings the most joy and fulfilment.

Fighting against the current is exhausting and rarely effective. We may be able to force some outcomes against the natural flow. But, at what cost to our energy levels, mental and physical health?

I for one have suffered immensely, whilst trying to swim upstream against the natural flow of events. I did it until I could no longer sustain the level of force required to push against what was happening.

In the ensuing, enforced rest period I learnt a lot. I had to pace myself in order to carry out even the smallest everyday tasks.

I was limited in what I could do each day, so I started to explore through reading, because it was the only thing I had enough energy for. I could watch television, but I found that boring and monotonous after a few weeks.

As I built up my energy reserves, I found there was a way to use less energy and actually achieve more. This was a huge surprise and a rather exciting discovery for me.

I was amazed again and again at the new possibilities which came my way with very little effort.

With space to rest, comes space to assess. Life always wants to show us the easy way forward. It just takes the willingness to look again, so you get to see life from an expanded viewpoint. Different perspectives start to reveal themselves.

Ultimately, we become surrendered when we are curious enough to look again, pretend we don't know, so we can see without an agenda.

This doesn't mean you can't have desires. But it is much more effective, if you allow your desires to guide you, and be flexible enough to be able to recognise the natural way forward.

Have your desire, then pay attention to see if it's in alignment with your natural flow. I now realise some of my desires aren't actually what I truly want. They are a representation of a need I have to be free. These days, when I have a desire, I let it go and then see where life takes me.

The more present I am and the more sustainable a present state of awareness becomes, the easier it is to discern which desires are in alignment with my highest desire of freedom.

My highest desire is my guiding light. Teamed up with my desire to serve, it leads me on a journey full of rewards, joy, and a deep level of fulfilment.

The Universe is designed to fulfil all our needs. We don't have to grab or push against the natural flow of events.

Our desires are wonderful and can be inspiring and motivating, driving us forward though life. But any desires which stem from our mind can be rather limiting. The mind can squash our imagination and intuition, so our desires can be quite small in actual fact.

The Universal force of love is flowing through us, always, in all ways. There is a grand vision which is so much greater than anything we could envisage.

To surrender an individual desire can lead to something far beyond anything we could dream up.

We're not surrendering to another being, as it sometimes feels. We're surrendering our individual sense of self to our big Self. Our Universal Self.

Our big Self knows the best and easiest path. When we can trust and go with what wants to happen, we can open up to a whole new perception of life.

If we shrink away from opportunities and avoid events, we could end up missing out on some potentially amazing possibilities.

Appearances can be deceiving. This reminds me of when I used to watch cartoons as a child. This big scary shadow would appear on the wall and the cat would squeal and run away. Then out toddles this tiny mouse. Hilarious!

We sometimes do this in our everyday lives. If the light of consciousness is dim and casts scary shadows, we may run away from the hidden opportunity.

When we pause and look again, we have a chance of seeing what is casting the shadow. The pure vision of what is happening, can be vastly different from the distorted shadow cast by the filters of the mind created by our belief system.

Always look again and take everything in. Allow 'what is' and get creative. What <u>can</u> you do? What small step can you take to move towards your desire?

Then be flexible. Be willing to change your approach or direction if the signs direct you in a different way.

Life will support your desires if they're in your best interests.

Go with the flow and let life show you the way. Let creativity flow through you to navigate a path through life which is joyful and fulfilling.

Surrender to the river of grace, let it carry you forward to a life you never even dreamed was possible...

"To the mind that is still
the whole Universe surrenders."

- Lao Tzu -

Chapter 24
Sweet Surrender

This whole book is about how surrender is good for the soul. How and why it will liberate you.

Surrender is the sweetest way to live your life.

Surrender leads to stillness > stillness leads to service > service leads to surrender.

When we can recognise how beneficial surrender can be, it becomes easier to apply. The small wins I gained when I first set out on a journey of surrender, motivated and inspired me to continue. Surrendering our own will to the universal will allows us to live in alignment with our highest desire.

Every time I surrender, I become more aware of stillness, silence, and space. This awareness of awareness is exquisite. We realise we are home and simply rest.

As we become acclimatised to our rested state of pure awareness, we are naturally empowered and motivated to serve others. It's as if our conscious awareness fills up with peace, love and joy. When we're full to the brim, it pours out into the people and world around us.

This act of service is enlivening, rewarding and delightful. I love to serve in any way I can.

My only side note to this is, to make sure you also look after your own needs. If you don't, life will become laboured, and you will run out of energy. You can't serve others if you're not thinking straight, you're sinking in a sea of emotion, or your body needs attention.

If we are still, we recognise what needs to be done, without having to think about it. We can serve others, look after ourselves and live a full, enjoyable life.

A path of service leads us back to our own heart, back to surrender. The more we give, the more we let go of. They all go hand in hand. Service, stillness, and surrender are the foundation of my life now. And it is oh so sweet!

I love giving! I'm gentle and considerate to myself and stillness is my priority. Everything else follows.

Anything I want comes from a still, silent state of surrender. The more I give without agenda or condition, the more I receive. The more I receive, the more I want to give, and the stiller I become. It is an upward spiralling path of joy!

Ten years ago, when I completed my 'mastery of the self' course in Spain, I was incredibly calm and happy. Five years ago, I was much more peaceful and joyful. A year ago, even more so. Today, as I write these words, I laugh at how small my experience of peace was a year ago, and how much greater it feels now.

Not much interferes with my peace or joy these days and if it does it's short lived. And yet... there's still more! There's always more. It boggles my mind! I cannot conceive of what joy and deepening peace lays ahead.

My experience is sweet and expansive. I also know if I continue to surrender this will only increase. The possibilities are infinite. There is no end or edge to my ever-expanding experience of peace and joy. My capacity for creativity has expanded with it. My resourcefulness has also grown.

If only I knew when I was a child, how much can be gained from surrender. I would likely not have been so stubborn! Stubborn, in my current experience is, a distortion of a one-pointed focus. It's detrimental to my health and well-being to be stubborn.

Surrender is definitely the way forward for me. There are still moments when I dig my heels in and argue with reality. Especially when it takes the form of a close family member!

My intent is always to surrender though, so all interactions are becoming easier to negotiate. All situations which arise are now navigated with much more ease and grace.

Surrender is always sweet, once we have let go of what we think should be happening and slip into the river of grace.

If you learn to flow with the natural course of events, you will also experience the sweetness of surrender.

"The moment you surrender to love and allow it
to lead you to exactly where your soul wants to go,
you will have no difficulty."

- Neale Donald Walsch -

Chapter 25
Ishani

Ishani is a Sanskrit word which means 'the love of God'. It is the female aspect of God and represents the divine feminine.

Sanskrit is an ancient language which is very pure and founded in the natural vibration of nature. Each Sanskrit word holds the essence of what it means. This makes it a powerful and transformational language to use. It also ensures we feel and are moved by using a Sanskrit word. As opposed to the majority of modern languages which are more intellectual. We can often get lost in the conceptual understanding, thereby missing the intended meaning and physiological impact of each word.

Ishani energy and the divine feminine are incredibly important in the world we live in today.

Masculine energy is still the dominant energy across the board in today's world view. Masculine energy is not bad or wrong, but it is most effective when working in harmony with feminine energy.

When the masculine and feminine are working together in harmony we create balance. Balance is grounding and centres us. It also allows for a greater degree of flexibility in my experience.

To harness the masculine energy and reach its greatest potential, we need to raise the feminine energy to work in synergy with it. This gives us the best chance of lifting this world out of its miserable slumber.

So many people are suffering and it's simply not necessary. The linear nature of the masculine is brilliant to drive action and get results. However, without a sufficient level of feminine energy, things become imbalanced and often head in the wrong direction.

Not wrong as in bad or failure, but in a way which does not serve all humanity to create in a loving and nurturing way.

The masculine energy could be depicted as the motor of a boat, which powers it to move forward at speed. The feminine energy could be depicted as the rudder, which directs the boat to change direction.

Feminine energy is best utilised for navigation, and masculine energy is best for creating and maintaining momentum.

In short, we need both the masculine and the feminine working together to get the most effective and beneficial results.

Feminine energy is receptive, nurturing, and intuitive. Masculine energy is inspiring, motivating, and conceptual.

This is not a battle between the sexes. Females are not better than males or vice versa. We all have a perfect balance of masculine and feminine energy within us. All it takes is to surrender to what wants to arise and manifest through us.

We will revert to our natural balance of masculine and feminine energy, when we stop trying to be someone who fits in and maintains the status quo.

We need to be daring and courageous so we can dance to our own beat.

This is not rebellion, it is empowerment.

Each one of us is equipped with the tools and insight to live the best version of ourselves. To create and produce what serves all of humanity.

I believe we must come away from a world view which rules and dominates others. We need to nurture our young and encourage them to follow their natural impulses. To dream big and believe in themselves. To work together and lift each other up, so we can all play our part.

The world is in turmoil. Yet I feel the tide is turning.

Mental health is starting to be addressed. It has to be. Nobody can take any more pressure. The overwhelm needs to be reduced. The best way to reduce overwhelm is to let people simply breathe and be themselves. To listen to each other and demonstrate we care.

When the pressure is off, then and only then, each person can start to explore who they are and what they want to do. What we naturally enjoy doing is the best way to discover our sense of purpose. Nothing need be forced. We don't have to do what we don't like. We all have different likes and tastes. Together we will cover all the bases If we nurture our natural talents.

Prejudice and judgement are holding us back. We are driving the world without direction founded in unconditional love.

Love must light the way. Love is the best compass.

Fear is not a clear directive. We run away, rather than run towards.

Fear is only in play when we forget who we really are. When you become present, fear fades away and love guides the way forward with the big picture in mind.

We can all let go a little bit more each day. Let go of the forcefulness, the need to be right, the lack of consideration for others and the environment.

Why?

Because all these things blind-side us. We lose clarity and the ability to respond positively to our external world.

The world isn't against us. It's just trying to nudge us towards the most beneficial outcome. If we can just let go and surrender our preconceived ideas, we will begin to see with more clarity what actually serves best in any given situation.

We need to utilise our feminine side to act in accordance with love. To regain a clear mind and recognise the clear path to a peaceful and happy world.

It is possible. I know it's possible because I already see it in play. We just need to connect the dots. Take a step back and pay attention, so clarity can resume.

We will always come back into balance when we pause, pay attention, look deeper and listen to each other.

Let go of your individual agenda. There is a way forward together. We don't need to argue or fight.

Mental health is a huge issue, because we are ignoring our inner voice of truth and love. We are trained to keep others happy, to follow rules, even when they make no sense to us.

What is our real objective?

I think we all want the same thing. We're just following archaic systems which no longer serve.

We need more freedom to do what we are meant to do. There is no opposition if we are all allowed to follow our intuition.

It would really help if we got out of our heads and into our hearts.

The thinking mind is linear, the heart is spatial. Our thinking is based on the past and misses the cues right in front of us. Whereas the heart sees without bias.

People are breaking down mentally because they are so far removed from their natural state where spatial awareness is valued as much as the linear mind.

We're thinking round and round in circles. Thinking also requires a huge amount of energy, so we're using all our energy up thinking with very little left to physically act.

We often can't implement our creative ideas because we're not sure if they will be successful.

Something needs to change if we want to live differently.

To come back into balance, the feminine energy must be given more credit and allowed to work its magic. For men as well as for women.

Some feminists, who are women but have often been aggressively masculine, try to force their way in the world. There was a time and a place for this. There are no mistakes. But now is the time to change tack and nurture ourselves. Powerful presence over forceful words and actions.

Presence is always the perfect balance of masculine and feminine. If we can be present now, let go of the past and future conceptual thinking and live in the now, we will be free to act in harmony with the natural and gentle underlying reality of love.

We can do this!

We can all be present. We can all let go of the past. We can all let the feminine rise within us to complement the masculine.

Surrender the way you've always done something, so you can discover the best way to act in <u>this</u> moment.

Let the feminine have a place in your life, to intuit the most creative and beneficial path forward.

You don't have to let go of the masculine, or make it wrong. Just make room for the feminine too. Value creativity as much as you value intellect. Let kids play and explore their own choices. Don't push someone to do something just because you think it's right for them.

Live your life the way you want to and let others live their life the way they want. We're all able to be our best selves when we're free to make our own choices.

Live and let live.

You may just find life gets easier and new, delightful possibilities open up for you. For your loved ones too, when you let them follow their own dreams.

We all know what is best for ourselves. Mistakes, or what appear to be mistakes, are the best learning tools.

Do whatever you feel you want to do and just don't care. Don't hold back and don't hold others back.

On the other side of fear is everything you ever wanted.

Let the divine feminine rise up and lead the way forward to the life of your dreams.

Yes.

This is possible.

You may need a tool to help guide you. I recommend Ascension, but follow your heart and go with whatever feels right for you!

"Be kind whenever possible.
It's always possible."

- Dalai Lama -

Chapter 26
True Compassion

I'm an Ishaya monk. Compassion is an important part of my life. We need more compassion in the world. Not just talk about it, but actually implement it in our everyday lives.

Compassion begins at home. It has to. If we're not compassionate with ourselves, there is no foundation for compassionate words and actions with others.

What do I mean by true compassion?

For me compassion is something which naturally occurs when you are present. Compassion is a combination of love and wisdom. It's a state of acceptance which blossoms into pure action, pure speech.

Compassion is rooted in this moment.

The mind chatter takes us away from this moment, and therefore away from compassion. We can have good intentions, but our words and actions can contribute to the problem if we're stuck in our heads.

Compassion is very different from sympathy. Typically, most people sympathise or judge. This is rarely helpful. it may have a temporary benefit if the other person can see you care. But we're way past the time when this is enough.

If you sympathise with someone it means you agree with their predicament. This is the same as jumping in the hole of misery that they are in. Now you have two people who are sad, angry fed up etc. What is the point of that?

They may feel less alone, but there is no need to remain in a pit of despair.

This is where compassion comes in.

Compassion is a different approach. Instead of jumping in the hole with your friends, family, or work colleagues, stay on the edge of the hole and drop a rope ladder down. Then invite them to climb up the ladder.

The act of compassion can play out in many different ways. It could mean simply listening to the other person. Not necessarily agreeing or disagreeing with them. Just making them feel seen, heard and accepted exactly as they are.

You may have something to say, but don't try to make them feel better. Don't try to fix them or change them.

Healing happens by itself. We all just need the space and rest to allow healing to happen. People are incredibly resourceful and capable of addressing their own feelings and challenges, if given the space and acceptance they need.

There may be something you can offer to help the person who is suffering. It is often more helpful to offer help with no expectation of them accepting it. It may not be best for them, or they may not be ready for it. They may not even recognise the help if they are lost in their emotion.

Always allow the other person to experience their feelings. Be there for them and supply tissues to mop the tears. They may need some physical help, or just a hug goes a long way in supporting them.

A hug or any physical touch may, however, be too much for them. If someone is overwhelmed, even a light touch may overload their system. Ask if they want a hug, rather than just giving them one. If you touch them to reassure them, pay attention to see if they freeze or tense. It may not be what they need. Your presence and acceptance may be enough to reassure and calm their state of turmoil.

Compassion can also be ruthless.

The best thing may be to say or do something which could appear harsh. Especially if they don't want to hear what you say or accept what you do. But it may be the one thing which shifts their mental and emotional state to a more relaxed and positive one.

For example, if a young child wants more sweets when they've already had quite a lot, a parent or caregiver would say no to more. The child just wants the sweets and can't take into account the previous amount consumed. More will likely lead to vomiting or health issues. The kindest thing to do is stop the supply of sweets.

The child will be angry and have a tantrum to try to persuade you to give them more. But a compassionate adult will stand their ground and say no. The child will hate it, but it's genuinely in their best interests.

Compassion is the path forward which is for the highest good for all. It doesn't consider what our ego wants. It is an option which brings us back into our natural state of peace.

Compassion may mean a temporary boundary needs to be put in place. The ego mind likes to control and will always go for the quick fix, even if it has unpleasant repercussions.

In contrast, compassion may mean not having an immediate chance to feel better or fulfil a desire in this moment. It creates space to come back to centre, to become aware and allow pure action to flow through.

Compassion is always in our best interests; it just may take a bit of time to recognise the benefit to us.

It does involve letting go. Surrendering the addictive impulse and allowing ourselves to rest.

There needn't be forcefulness or rigidity though. If someone is in a hole, you drop down the ladder and they refuse to climb out, leave them there. Bring care packages and love them just as they are.

Stand your ground and honour your own useful boundaries. Honour other people's boundaries too. Even if it is causing them harm. Sometimes people have to reach rock bottom and stay there for long enough to motivate them in making a change for the better.

Everyone has the right to their own choices. We can suggest a course of action, then let them choose if it is what they want or not.

We are all capable of making our own choices.

Obviously, there are times when intervention is necessary to prevent long term or irreparable damage. But mostly, it's important to let people, even young children, make mistakes so they can learn for themselves.

Compassion is a gentle thing. It is empowering, kind and liberating.

Surrender, be compassionate and let's change this world for the better.

"Filling the conscious mind with ideal conceptions is a characteristic of Western theosophy, but not the confrontation with the shadow and the world of darkness.

One does not become enlightened by imagining figures of light, but by making the darkness conscious."

- Carl Jung -
The collected works of Carl Jung - Vol 13 - page 335

Chapter 27
The Light of Consciousness

Consciousness is simply awareness. To be fully aware, consciously aware of everything, every part of your Self, is a powerful thing.

The term Enlightenment is often used to describe this fully aware state of being. Enlightenment can sound like an unreachable goal for spiritual seekers only. However, it is not elusive, it's absolutely attainable in this lifetime for every person in existence. You must want it though and be willing to go for it with 100% commitment.

This doesn't mean it needs to be hard work or difficult to attain. In truth it's easy. It just requires a one-pointed focus and the desire to make it more important than anything else. Enlightenment is our natural state of being. Therefore, the approach is all about keeping it simple and easy.

We're not going anywhere; we're not adding or subtracting anything. It simply involves getting to know your Self. Because it's our natural state to be fully aware, we can access it in the blink of an eye.

There are many times in our lives when we slip into this full state of awareness and become present to the moment as it unfolds.

For example, when we're immersed in nature, in awe of something or totally engaged with all our attention on the task in hand. When we cease thinking and gain absolute clarity and focus.

Enlightenment is when the light of conscious awareness is fully engaged. Again, it's completely natural and therefore easy to do. Which is why we can easily slip into this state without trying.

What then prevents us from experiencing this awake state of conscious awareness in our everyday lives?

Habit. That's it. Habit. It's the only reason we aren't all experiencing life from a state of full conscious awareness.

The habit is to think, to identify with the thoughts arising within and flowing through our conscious awareness.

We've learnt to identify with an idea, a conclusion we've come to and believed is true. Once we believe a thought is true, we download it into our unconscious mind and it becomes a filter, a point of reference to refer to.

A belief is just a fleeting thought, an idea which we subscribe to. A judgement which is held onto and therefore governs our experience. When we do this, identification begins, and we lose the capacity to choose for something different.

One thought held onto is the unconscious mind, acts like a magnet, and more beliefs are downloaded creating a programme. A programme which becomes a thought generator, and the ego mind is firmly in place.

The mind affects how we see, hear, feel, and experience everything. And I mean everything. Who we believe we are, how we speak, act, and interact with our world, how we perceive the world and the people in it. All this is governed by the mind.

The mind appears to be all powerful, but in truth it is just a collection of thoughts which operate in the shadows. Sometimes referred to as the shadow self.

We cannot control how we think until we become conscious of these underlying thought patterns. When we become consciously aware of them, then we have a choice, we can choose again.

This shadow self has been given a bad reputation. It's often portrayed as if it's the worst part of ourselves. This simply isn't true. The shadow self is just made up of the parts we have classified as bad, wrong, or unacceptable.

Typically, the classification happened because our caregivers demonstrated through words or actions that these parts weren't acceptable or welcome.

Over time, we learnt to suppress everything deemed unwanted or unacceptable to keep ourselves safe and or loved. Suppression developed into the unconscious version - repression, which became an automatic response to aggressive, controlling, or manipulative people.

The shadow self is a part of us. It's not bad or wrong at all. In fact, often the parts of ourselves we learnt to hide away are our best, most useful assets. Our unique talents and skills, which are desperately needed in the world right now. We need every person to uncover their shadow self, embrace and harness it so they can be the best version of themselves.

We need to make the darkness conscious, so we can operate at full capacity and make a positive difference, for us and for everyone else.

Just like when we turn on the light in a dark room. As soon as the light is turned on, the darkness dissipates, and we can see the contents clearly. We can move about the room more easily and see what needs to be done.

In this same way, we can turn on the light of consciousness, so we can see who we really are. Who we are beyond the minds idea of who we think we are.

This is liberation. This is how we are meant to live our lives.

The only thing in the way of the light being turned on is a thought. In truth, the thought is not actually in the way. It just diverts our attention away from reality, which effectively turns the light down, so we can't see beyond the content of the thought.

We are the light. We are pure consciousness. To directly experience this awakened state, we need only surrender the thought and pay attention. The light flips on and we are awake. Or, more accurately, we become aware of the light.

It's very simple and easy to replicate for each and every one of us. We just have to want it and detach from all the thoughts long enough to see they are just a fleeting idea.

When we do this, our conscious awareness expands beyond the content of thought to include the context of pure awareness. Also known as becoming present.

Present to the fullness of the moment. Everything goes back into context, and we experience this presence as gentleness and ease.

Enlightenment is easy, it's a down to earth and natural experience. It's the birthright of all of humanity, and it's accessible now.

It can be a slow process to cultivate the habit of keeping the light of consciousness on though. Most people require a tool and guidance from someone who has already established the habit to remain awake.

The tool I use is Ascension and I have a Teacher who guides me to cultivate the habit of presence. I pay it forward and guide others who are starting off on their journey to become present.

We're all in this together, walking each other home.

To remain fully awake. To be the light of consciousness and transform this world through love, kindness, and acceptance.

"The closest, nearest, and dearest place to commune with Truth is within yourself."

- Sadhguru -

Chapter 28
Absolute Truth

We all have our own perspective on life, our own version of the truth. We see life as we are and rarely how it truly is. Everyone has a different take on the events we witness and the situations we experience. Our outlook on life defines the experience we have.

We argue with others based on our world view. Our truth is <u>the</u> truth. But it isn't. Everything is subjective, based on the subject, the person who is having the experience.

Nothing is ever set in stone. Truth is malleable and changeable as life evolves. What is true for you today may not be true for you tomorrow. What is true for someone else, may not be true for you.

In the relative world, change is the only constant.

Even the underlying reality of everything in existence, which is the only permanent thing, holds the potential for many different outcomes and experiences, so our experience of it continually changes.

Truth is fluid and thank goodness for that! Without this changeable experience, life would be dull. The absolute truth, in my experience, is there is no absolute truth.

Life is ever-changing and fluid. If we hold on to our version of truth, life can got bumpy really fast. People clash with each other when they do this.

In a present surrendered state of being, it is possible to move with the changing landscape and recognise what serves best for this moment in time.

It is also just as easy to let a solution go and realise the best solution is now a different one. It is incredibly freeing to develop a surrendered state of being. You no longer need to hold onto any idea as a truth. You can roll with the changes and see the way forward with clarity and grace.

I've also developed a high level of trust. I don't need to stick with my own choices. Well, most of the time! If I'm with someone and they choose differently from me, it's now much easier to surrender my vision and go along with theirs.

This has revolutionised my life. The rigidity of holding on to my version of truth was tiring, pressure filled and limiting. My clarity has refined as I've learnt to surrender my perception as a relative truth and be open to what someone else suggests. Or even to what the unfolding events present as a previously unrecognised possibility.

Truth is an unfolding, ever-changing flow. We never need hold on to any idea. If we do hold on, it's essentially like moving through life with blinkers on. We'll only see what our version of the truth allows us to see.

I don't know about you, but I like to be open to other possibilities. I'm a free spirit who doesn't like to be tethered, but I previously had no idea the tether was within my mind. I always believed other people were controlling me. As I've grown in consciousness, the inner tether became visible to me, and I let it go.

I still get blind-sided sometimes. This is usually a temporary glitch in the matrix these days. I quite quickly recognise where the control and limitation are coming from, and I ride the wave of emotion until it subsides, and a greater level of clarity arises within my experience.

Not only is this new capability to be open and fluid beneficial for me, but it is also of great value for maintaining harmonious relationships.

Everyone wants to be valued, so the capacity to go with another choice, to allow their version of truth to be the guiding light is a huge gift.

Surrender has been the greatest factor in cultivating the ability to be open to the changing landscape of my life.

Whatever I believe to be true I surrender, again and again. So less and less distorts my perception and clouds my clarity.

Even if I recognise a clear way forward I (mostly) don't need to stick with it. There can still be a slight lag in my ability to recognise a course correction is required to stay on the most beneficial path. But sometimes I can turn on a sixpence and instantly go with the flow to accommodate for arising circumstances.

My closest relationships are my greatest handicap. The places where I'm most likely to dig my heels in. It's wonderful to recognise the areas where I'm going to trip up. It makes it much less likely to happen when I'm aware. It also allows me to spot it in the moment of stubborn resistance and be willing to surrender my belief, so I can be open to other possibilities.

It's still a work in progress, but I've reached a level of clarity and willingness which makes life so much easier and more delightful.

Surrender will remain as my guiding principle because I'm excited to see what else is possible. I'm also curious to witness life unfold without the limitations of relative truths.

When I have no agenda, no need for a particular outcome in each and every moment. What then?

Then… the big 'T' Truth is revealed. This Truth is an experience, not an idea. It cannot be described. Absolute Truth is boundless, formless, and infinite. It condemns no-one and lifts the veil of illusion, so life is seen and experienced in its purity, in unity and compassion.

The absolute Truth does not require our agreement. It is beyond personal choice. It will remain untouchable waiting quietly for our recognition. All the kicking and screaming in the world will have no impact on Truth.

But …when we become quiet, surrender to the moment, we rest in stillness and are able to recognise that Truth is here, now and will never leave us.

Let's surrender our relative truths together and allow the Universe to show us more. To reveal the absolute Truth and live a life in wonder and awe.

"Loneliness is a sign you are
in desperate need of yourself."

- Rupi Kaur -

Chapter 29
Divine Connection

We all want connection, a sense of belonging and acceptance. We look for it in our relationships and in the groups we belong to. It really helps to connect with others, especially if they're like-minded, kind, and friendly.

However, these connections will always be affected by the relationship we have with our Self. I don't mean with the ego self, I mean the big self with a capital S.

The ego self is just an idea or opinion we have about who we are. The ego self is a reflection of all the conclusions and beliefs we've learnt are who we are and therefore hold onto in the unconscious mind. None of them are true. They are only ideas, conclusions we have previously drawn, based on the information and feedback we received as a young child.

The real you is the pure awareness which houses and is aware of the ideas and conclusions. It is unaffected by them and continues to exist in its pure untainted wholeness, regardless of what we think and do.

It is such a huge relief to recognise this. Not because someone tells you it is so, but because you have accessed the direct experience underlying this concept.

When you come to recognise the real you and begin to rest as this pure awareness, you connect with your divine Self. This divine Self is intuitive and needs nothing from the perceived outside. There isn't actually an outside, there is no separation. The Self is complete and whole unto itself.

To be able to surrender the ego self, so you can regain a conscious awareness of your divinity, is a beautiful and fulfilling experience.

What you're actually surrendering, is a distorted version of reality, as seen through the filters of the mind - the ego. You're surrendering the ego, so you can be your real Self, your divine Self.

As you begin to realise who you really are, you are able to experience every moment fresh and brand new. Nothing gets boring. Everything is fascinating and alive.

You're not surrendering to someone or something else. You're surrendering a pretend version of you to the real you. The limited (little) self to the big Self. The fake, albeit 'real feeling' self, to the true Self.

Life will never be the same again. Can you take a chance on an alternate reality? What have you got to lose? Pain, misery, boredom, fear... Yes! You will lose it all.

In the space which is left, you will emerge, pure, unadulterated you. Along with this pure, original you, will come a whole different operating mode. One founded in love, intuition, and ease.

Then what?... You'll never suffer again.

Everything, everything is happening to help you wake up. Wake up and be yourself, so you can play your part to heal the word and make it a better place to live.

Divine means Godlike. The word God can put some people off, because so many religions use the word God as if it is a separate being.

This is not how I mean the word divine.

For me divine represents the highest state of consciousness a human can attain. It is not something outside of us, it's an inner state of wholeness. We experience it when we unify every part of ourselves.

Acceptance of everything we think we are, allows us to stop trying to be something else and simply rest. Rest in our true nature and discover the truth of who we are, without the mind's opinions influencing our experience.

This is a pure state. An original state. A state where you aren't subscribed to any idea or opinion. Nothing dictates who you are. Paying attention without dialogue reveals this still, silent, pure state of awareness.

It's very simple and can be easy. We just need to pay attention and stay attentive. The habit is to follow thought and identify with the content. Therefore, it's really helpful to have a tool, a technique to redirect your attention back onto itself.

Then you can experience what divine really means. Beyond, way beyond, any conceptual understanding you've learnt about the word.

This is freedom.

To shed all concepts and come back to the direct experience. Come back to your own divinity.

Loneliness will then become an alien concept, which bears no relation to your experience. The completeness of pure conscious when fully engaged, leaves no room left for loneliness, doubt, confusion, or worthlessness.

From this foundation, every relationship becomes easy and heartfelt. Including the relationship we have with ourselves.

Do you want to taste the chocolate … or just think about it?

I want the taste, to have the direct experience, not just talk, think, or fantasise about eating chocolate!

I want to discover and rest in my own divinity. I have tasted it and I want more... I want to know what it's like to live my entire life from this pure, original, natural state of being.

I'm going for it... will you join me?

"But man's task is ... to become conscious of the contents that press upward from the unconscious. Neither should he persist in his unconsciousness, nor remain identical with the unconscious elements of his being, thus evading his destiny, which is to create more and more consciousness."

- Carl Jung -
Memories, Dreams, Reflections

Chapter 30
Cosmic Exploration

You may have read this book and thought:

"I know all this!"

It is likely you do know some or even most of it. The knowledge, however, has no intrinsic value without the means and willingness to implement it.

You will also need to find ways to apply it practically in your everyday life.

The good news is the means to implement my suggestions will be accessed through gaining a present state of awareness.

Not just thinking about it or applying it some of the time. To truly experience all that is available to you, it is necessary to connect the dots and remain present in every moment of your day-to-day existence. To apply the knowledge to its fullest potential.

Feedback is invaluable, as you practise implementing the knowledge. But you don't need any more information to actually apply the theory and put it into practise. You just need to do it!

Action leads to learning, but learning doesn't necessarily lead to action.

Surrender is an ongoing journey of exploration. The exploration begins, and ends, as an inner cosmic journey of discovery and realisation.

Are you with me?

The journey within has no ending. It is an expanding path which always leads to more. And it gets more exciting, joyful, and meaningful the more we explore. It certainly does in my experience, and I'm sure it will for you as well.

It's helpful to maintain an innocent approach, to be continually curious and open to what wants to be revealed.

Close your eyes and simply observe what is here right now. Use a technique to refine your awareness, to anchor you in the here and now, when your mind wanders off down the proverbial rabbit hole.

I use, and will continue to use, the Ascension techniques as taught by The Bright Path Ishayas. For me they work beautifully. The mechanical nature and structure of these techniques brings me back 100% of the time no matter how lost in thought I am.

This keeps it effective, simple, and easy. I love that! No effort required. No belief. Nothing. Just the willingness to close the eyes and use Ascension to expand your conscious awareness of the still, silent, space within.

I consider myself a Cosmic Explorer. I'm motivated and excited to continue exploring my inner landscape.

As I explore with my eyes closed, I deepen my connection and activate surrender. This then reflects in my everyday life with my eyes open.

The more still I become, the more fulfilling, rewarding, and easy my life becomes.

I get more curious as each new day arrives... What else is possible? What else?

If something feels hard, uncomfortable, confusing, or disturbing I no longer try to push the experience away. Not consciously any way! I still occasionally catch myself resisting. It's only difficult when I slip back into unconsciously resisting. As I've said before, when it gets hard, get curious!

Thankfully, it gets easier and easier to spot. When I see it, I celebrate, get curious and continue to explore.

In order to explore, I get out of my head and into the body. When it is difficult, painful, disturbing, confused, I ask myself: What is the physical, visceral body sensation I'm experiencing?

Then I watch. I observe until the observer becomes one with the observed and the unified experience reveals all I need to surrender.

Surrender is a path of freedom, not a path to freedom. The surrendered state is a liberating, joyful, peaceful state.

It's everything I've ever wanted... and more

There's always more!

Other books by the author

Peace or Pain: Discovering the unbroken you and changing your relationship with pain

The purpose of this book is to let everyone know that they are not broken and do not need fixing. Peace or pain is a choice that is possible for everyone in each and every moment. It might not seem possible to you right now, but it is, and this book will open your eyes to how you can change your relationship with pain. Physical, mental, and emotional pain.

. . .

Peace or Pain Journal - coming soon

To support you in your bid to reduce suffering and increase peace, this journal has a card deck in the back part of the book to inspire and guide you in your exploration. The journal pages have boxes to fill in and questions to answer to raise alertness and bring more awareness into your discoveries. The more conscious you become the more you will change your relationship with pain, ease suffering and connect with inner peace.

. . .

Peace or Pain Audios - coming soon

These audios work together to bring you into the direct experience of peace, release the tension in your body and cultivate conscious awareness. Listening to these guided meditations and exercises can have a profound impact from the first time you hear them. Consistently listening to them will allow you to transform the conceptual understanding into a direct living experience.

Resources

Ascension: To find a course or discover more about the Ascension techniques and teaching of The Bright Path Ishayas please visit the website: www.thebrightpath.com

Reviews: If you have found the contents of this book helpful, please leave a review on Amazon to help others find this book.

Share: Please let others know about this book or buy them a copy. Together we can change the world!

Videos and Webinars: Available on the YouTube channel 'Boundless Meditation'. Please subscribe, like and share with friends, colleagues and family who may also benefit from watching these videos.

Podcasts/Seminars/YouTube/Television: Meera is open to appearing on any platform to talk about a variety of topics. E.g. Peace or Pain is a choice; Reducing Stress; The Art of Surrender; Emotions; Consciousness.

If you would like Meera to come and give a talk, an interview, or facilitate a workshop please email her at: info@boundless-meditation.co.uk

Website: All resources, courses and links available here: www.boundless-meditation.co.uk

Facebook Group: Peace or Pain, join to stay connected.

About the author

Originally a Graphic Designer, Meera has been a Bright Path Ishaya monk and teacher of Ascension since 2012.

Meera is dedicated to helping people discover who they really are and how to make the choice for freedom. As part of her own journey, she has discovered that anything is possible and wants others to know how easy and practical it can be to live a happy and full life free from suffering.

Meera is the author of Peace or Pain - Discovering the unbroken you and changing your relationship with pain. She is currently working as a Meditation Tutor for City Lit in London and online, as well as teaching courses to learn the Ascension techniques with The Bright Path Ishayas. Meera also offers 1-2-1 sessions, workshops and courses for pain management, meditation tuition and a variety of other topics.

She has many more books planned - a Peace or Pain Journal and set of audios to go with her first book; a book for parents about relationship issues and the worries we have about our children which includes how to experience peace in amongst all the chaos of family life; and many more topics to support people in addressing the common issues we experience in the hectic, dysfunctional modern-day life.

Meera lives in Hertfordshire, near London in the UK with her family and two cats.

Peace or Pain

Chapter 1
Desperation

How did I get here?

'Here' is on my kitchen floor, sitting down in a crumpled heap. I'm holding a knife in my hand and I'm thinking of cutting my wrist and ending it all. I wasn't really thinking about dying. I just wanted the pain to stop. I was silently screaming inside myself.

"Why does this hurt so much? Why won't the pain stop? I need it to stop. I can't take any more."

Nobody realised how much it hurt. Nobody could make it stop. Nobody.

. . .

My husband was crouched down beside me, a terrified look in his eyes. I knew he loved me, and I knew he would do anything for me. But what good is that when nothing can be done.

He was talking softly to me, trying to get me to put the knife down. I could tell he was scared to say the wrong thing, or get too close in case it made me use the knife. I was sorry to put him through this, but I was so desperate. I literally could take no more pain at that moment.

I was vaguely aware that he was holding our son in his arms, but I hadn't looked away from the knife since I had collapsed on the floor. It had taken a great deal of effort to get here, because I was unable to walk without assistance. I couldn't lift my right leg at all and could only get my left leg an inch off the floor, so I had dragged myself on crutches just to get here.

My condition is called Symphysis Pubis Dysfunction (SPD). It is a fairly rare condition, which started in the pregnancy of our second child. The child my husband was holding right now. I just had an ache in my hip to start with, which I told my midwife about. I was told not to complain, that I'd had a child before and should know you get aches and pains as part of the process. Except I hadn't experienced any aches or pains in my first pregnancy.

My first pregnancy was easy. This was new, but I felt that I was making a fuss, so I kept quiet and carried on in silence. The ache got a bit worse and a few other places started to hurt too, but it wasn't too bad, so I stayed quiet.

It wasn't until I was about 32 weeks pregnant that my legs collapsed from underneath me and I fell over. Then I was told, I should have said something earlier. That was rather infuriating obviously, because I had said something. I was given little to no help because there was apparently nothing that could be done. I have since learnt that this is not entirely true.

I had a pair of crutches left over from a sprained ankle. They were mismatched and very old, but they served the function I required. So I hobbled and dragged my pregnant body around until I gave birth to a healthy bundle of joy. A son we called Brodie. He was of course adorable, and we loved him from the minute we saw him, just the same as we did our daughter Jasmine.

Now I had given birth I could at least get physiotherapy to try to heal and recover from the SPD. I was pushed and manipulated by several physiotherapists, to try to get my pelvis back into its original alignment. To no avail, I stayed twisted.

After about 6 months I went on to try Osteopathy, which gradually untwisted my pelvis over the course of a year. Just as it was almost straight, it shifted the other way, then pulled apart and stayed that way. That was when the pain got worse and shifted to my back as well as the front and right side of my pelvis.

You have no idea how much this hurt, and it only continued to get more and more painful by the day. At this point I gave up on a solution and resigned myself to a life of pain. My mum still looked though, and we went through a whole host of options, some of which helped, but not enough to make a difference to my quality of life.

So here I am on my kitchen floor, knife in hand. I was at the end of my tether. There were no more options available and I could not live like this anymore.

Then my son made a sound. He had been silent up until that point, so I had barely noticed him in my anguished state.

I looked up, straight into his eyes and just stared, captivated by my son's gaze. Something shifted in me. It was like I took a step out of time. Everything else faded away and it was like I could see the whole Universe in his eyes. It was an indescribable experience. Nothing mattered in that moment. There was only a profound stillness that stretched to eternity. It was so full of an exquisite still, silent presence that it was beyond words. My mind was blown away and the experience was all there was. Peace. A seemingly endless sea of peace and a silent wisdom, that was such a pure experience I could not look away. I was completely transfixed.

It had a hugely profound effect on me. There was hope. I didn't know what it was, but I knew there was hope. There was hope that things could change, that things could be different. Then my mind kicked in again and thoughts of what I had nearly done flooded in.

I was so ashamed that I had done this in front of my son. What effect would this have on him. I came to my senses. My husband saw the change in me and gently, but as swiftly as he dared, he took the knife from my grasp.

It was then, in that moment, that my whole life started all over again. I had to find a way to beat this. If I couldn't do it for myself, I could do it for my son. He was here after all. I was lucky to have him.

I felt the gratitude for the gift he was. I felt the love pouring out of his small, but powerful body. There was such innocence and trust that was so pure and clear. It was beautiful.

I could do this; I could find a way to be well and walk again. I had to at least try. I owed him this much. I chose to live. For my son, for my daughter, for my husband and most importantly, for myself.

I also wanted to find out what the transcendent experience was all about. If I could access an all-encompassing peace in such a distressing moment, surely I could find it again…

Printed in Great Britain
by Amazon

26762945R00106